The Teaching Assistant's Guide to ADHD

T0353238

The Teaching Assistant's Guide to ADHD

Kate Spohrer

continuum

Continuum International Publishing Group

The Tower Building   80 Maiden Lane
11 York Road   Suite 704
London, SE1 7NX   New York, NY 10038

www.continuumbooks.com

British Library Cataloguing-in-Publication Data
A catalogue record for this book is available from the British Library.

ISBN: 9-780-8264-8375-1 (paperback)

Typeset by Kenneth Burnley, Wirral, Cheshire

Contents

Acknowledgements

Thanks go to all of the families I have worked with and learned so much from. Thanks also to my mother and son, without whose inspiration and support this book would not have been possible. Thanks also to Jessica Kingsley Publishers for allowing the quotation from *Marching to a Different Tune*.

Introduction:
How to use this book

I have written this book with a view to it being scanned from cover to cover, with more time being taken on the areas that are of particular interest and relevance to the reader. My recommendation would be to ensure completion of the activities and the quizzes which appear at the end of each chapter. At the back of the book the quizzes appear plus suggested answers and comments. I hope you will have a go at the quizzes before you look at the suggested answers! This is because it will be a much better learning experience for you if you do.

Throughout this book for the sake of ease of reading the pronoun 'he' has been used.

This book aims to help the reader

- become familiar with the criteria for diagnosis
- consider the implications of the label AD/HD
- consider the implications of having an AD/HD-type personality
- look at possible causes for AD/HD and gain some understanding of the associated behaviour
- gain understanding of the special nature of AD/HD and its effects on a child and their family
- become aware of the range of therapies that may help
- provide some practical in-school strategies that can be used immediately

Note to the reader

Although the official title of this book uses the terminology ADHD without the slash, within the book you will find AD/HD with the slash used. This is not a typographical error, it is simply that the term AD/HD has been the official label following the last diagnostic criteria update and it is therefore technically appropriate to use AD/HD. However, it is felt that most people know the term ADHD, and that in this world of search engines the more commonly used ADHD would reach a wider audience – after all a book that is never read is no use to anyone, is it?

1

What is AD/HD?

This chapter

- explains the definition and diagnostic criteria of AD/HD
- describes what AD/HD may look like in school

What is AD/HD?

Can you think of a time when you acted impulsively or absent-mindedly and did something you wish you hadn't, or omitted to do something you wish you had? Were you able to learn from that event and modify your behaviour afterwards, or did it take a few attempts before you had your behaviour under your control? If you were able to modify your behaviour straight away you are lucky, if it took you a few more attempts you are probably pretty much like the majority of people, but if you still are finding difficulty after a long time trying, you might well be very interested in reading on. Even if you didn't, I hope you will read on for the sake of the young people you work with.

Case studies

Welcome to the world of Harry Hectic, Willy and Wendy Whizz and Darren Dream and friends.

Let me introduce you to our virtual group. The pupils in the group are of mixed ages all in mainstream school. Read through and see if any of the children have similarities to children you work with. Even if the children are of ages you do not currently work with, it is a good idea to read through the case studies as this could be the child you are working with in the future, or were in the past, and it all helps to increase understanding of this personality type.

Harry

Harry is in Year 6 now and although doing well in school was a trial to his teachers when younger. He is a whiz on computer games and good at art and story writing, but doesn't like doing either of them. He is good academically, but doesn't find it easy to get started on any work, his written work output can be low and his teachers have sometimes felt frustrated by this because they feel he has ability. Orally he is able to converse at an age appropriate or above level and can 'talk the hind leg off a donkey'.

His mum reports she has always had difficulty with him behaviourwise. He was a poor sleeper and had to have medication to help him sleep as a young child. She also says he was always on the go and demanding to be taken out until he got into computer games, with which he seems to be obsessed now – spending most of his time glued to a screen.

He likes to play with friends, but seemed to find friendships hard to strike up. His mum had to work hard generating situations where he could play with friends.

Sometimes Harry drives everyone around him mad because he seems to become obsessed with something – usually something he wants to do, or to get – for a while, then he will suddenly have forgotten all about it and be focusing – or distracted by – something completely different.

Darren

Darren is in Year 8. He seems to be in a world of his own. Darren will come into the classroom and, if allowed would sit at the back, look as though he was working, but in fact produce negligible work. Darren is in lower sets for maths, English and science. His teacher has noticed that he has coped very well with mathematical problems involving spatial awareness, in fact he is the best in the group in this area. He appears to have some dyslexic tendencies in that his spelling and handwriting are poor he receives some extra support from the special needs department for these learning needs.

He can be engaged in sensible, relevant conversation, but when you catch him chatting to his peers it is rarely about the task set.

Darren finds organizing his stuff difficult, he rarely has the appropriate equipment with him, this causes him to get detentions which seem to have no impact on improving his organization whatsoever.

A number of teachers have expressed concern about Darren's slowness, they are perplexed because although slow he doesn't seem to lack ability.

Willy

Willy in Year 3, is a twin to Wendy and has been described by some as eccentric. He is a dreamer and will frequently try to engage adults in conversation completely irrelevant to the task set. He has high levels of interest and knowledge in some fields, particularly birds and animal life.

Willy likes to fiddle with something at all times, in fact he seems to need to do this to be able to work on anything his teacher sets him.

His work output is below that expected from a boy of his ability. He reports he finds a lot of the work boring, and accepts that his interest wanders to subjects inside his head rather than the lesson.

Willy's parents report that he is a poor sleeper, and that they have to keep him occupied at home if they want any peace. Consequently Willy's father is always on the lookout for activities that Willy might enjoy doing, and is willing to take him to as many as he can fit in.

His teachers have reported that they have to repeat instructions several times to Willy before he will begin a task. He also drifts off the task very quickly.

His parents feel that some of his teachers in the past victimized Willy and did not try to understand what sort of child he is. His parents feel he is a very able boy, but the school feel he is average to above rather than gifted.

Willy does possess a vivid imagination and, if given a tape recorder to dictate onto, can tell some good stories. Willy also enjoys model making and can get very absorbed in such projects.

Wendy

Wendy, Willy's twin sister, is in Year 3; she is a lively and loud child. Many describe her as a tomboy, she much prefers to play with boys than girls. In nursery school she was constantly running about and shouting. She is still very active and shouts out a lot in class, and although what she says is often relevant and a correct answer to a question, she does not get much recognition for her thinking because she has not mastered classroom conventions such as raise your hand before speaking. Her tray is always in a mess, her appearance is dishevelled and her work is untidy.

Her teacher has had her mother into school on several occasions to discuss her behaviour. Her mother feels rather 'got at' by the school and thinks it's hard enough dealing with her at home, let alone being troubled by the school's problems.

Her mother has reported that she demands a lot of attention at home. Although only young she has shown a somewhat precocious attitude towards boys of her own and slightly older age.

Wendy finds it a trial to write things down so doesn't show her full potential in her written work. She enjoys communicating through art and talking, and she has also shown some ability in dance. Maths is a pet hate of Wendy's – she thinks it is 'boring'.

Amina

Amina is in Year 6 and a constant fidget and talker in class. Her teachers feel she has average to above average ability, but a problem in reaching what the school consider to be her potential, particularly where pen and paper tasks are involved. She seems to compensate for the lack of academic achievement which everyone around her expects her to achieve by sexually precocious behaviour and showing off to try to engender peer acceptance.

Amina took part in a project where relaxation exercises were practised regularly each week. Her teacher noticed that during these sessions she found it impossible to keep still and quiet – 'there was always a little rustling or whispering when Amina was with us'.

Ellie

Ellie is in Year 7. On the outside Ellie can appear quiet, shy and withdrawn. On the inside she would love to express herself but somehow just can't summon up the confidence to do so. She will go into class and sit at the back keeping away from the action. She is likely to be ignored by people because she looks stand-offish and aloof. She tends to make few friends, and prefers them to be from outside school. She appears to find it difficult to interact with her peers. She interacts better with adults or children of a different age to herself and tends to prefer the company of boys, finding 'girly' group activities abhorrent and dreads break and lunchtime. Academically she never seems to excel, finding it difficult to pay attention to detail, but always does well enough to get by. Her teachers tend to leave her alone most of the time. Sometimes she feels she would like to be encouraged into being more extrovert as she doesn't have the confidence to go it alone.

Steven

Steven is in Year 6 and a trial to his teachers. He is a whiz on computers, but his handwriting is described as atrocious, his written work output is very low and his teachers feel frustrated by this because they feel he has ability. Orally he is able to converse at an age appropriate or above level and can 'talk the hind leg off a donkey'.

His mum reports she has always had difficulty with him behav-iourwise, he was a poor sleeper and had to have medication to help him sleep as a young child. She also says he is always taking things apart, like radios and speakers, and putting them back together successfully.

Steven himself gets into a lot of trouble at school. He is always fiddling with something, or tapping or quietly humming away to himself, but he has an ally in one of the teachers who believes he has a lot of talent if only it can be channelled. She works hard to persuade the other staff at the school that this is the case, but even she at times feels like giving up on him.

Steven does not like art, finds spelling difficult and often loses his stuff.

John

John has shown increasingly difficult behaviour at home and at school over the last year. John is now in Year 5. His class over the years have suffered from a number of staff changes due to illness and staff gaining positions in other schools. John is not the only child in the class requiring extra-special attention.

John has inattentive and impulsive behaviour, he will walk out of the classroom if he doesn't like what he has been asked to do. John is average to above average ability, but is reluctant to take any risks with his learning, so is operating at a level below that expected.

John's dad has a very impulsive and inattentive temperament. He has a drink problem and has been detained at Her Majesty's pleasure in the past. The family live in a small house which opens straight onto a busy road. There are four children in the family of which John is the oldest.

John himself has been in trouble with the police, and he has also set fire to things in the house causing his family great distress.

John has been diagnosed AD/HD and took Ritalin for a while, but it did not suit him. John has a statement for special educational needs which provides 15 hours a week support time, but the school feel they are failing John in the support they provide because they feel they are not making any progress. His teacher and TA would like to have more contact with the Child and Adolescent Mental Health Service (CAMHS) and the Youth Offending Team so that they could all work together to the same aim, but they are finding communication difficult at the moment.

Kabir

Kabir is in Year 9. He has a diagnosis for AD/HD and has been taking Ritalin for a short time, although the dose has recently been increased because the effects appeared to be wearing off.

Kabir has had difficulties in school and at home for a long time. In primary school he was disruptive in class: shouting out, swearing, going off task, engaging in conversation with other pupils when he and they should have been working. At home his mother reports he has always been very lively, needing lots of her attention.

He showed a lot of talent in the dance and drama field. He also enjoys art. To begin with he settled into the high school quite well, but the staff gradually became exasperated with his behaviour which was becoming more and more disruptive. This precipitated his mother taking him for an AD/HD assessment.

Kabir has never been malicious, he is described as charming and a boy you just can't fail to see the nice side of, but in the classroom he is a real trial. He is of average to above average ability, but is underperforming in school. Kabir is at risk of permanent exclusion for his persistently disruptive behaviour. Kabir's mum is supportive of the school, but also feels privately that the school are not accepting Kabir for the person he is.

Jim

Jim is in Year R. He has been attending school since nursery. He has always stood out in the classroom as being a bit of a whirlwind. Jim is partial to daubing paint on other children and furniture, he pulls hair, leaves taps running, throws stones at cars in the school car park. Although very accomplished orally he is slow to start reading. His mother reports that instead of walking he runs everywhere, and will climb on walls if he can get the chance. He still sucks a dummy at night and before school. He also seems to dribble quite a bit. She also reports that he gets angry and frustrated when he can't do something, not just when he is told he can't do something, but when he can't physically do something. She says he talks incessantly at home, and always wants her to play with him. He doesn't settle well to many activities, preferring to quickly move on from one thing to another.

In class he likes to change activity quickly, he shouts out frequently, trying to engage the teacher in conversation without any regard for other pupils' needs. He recently got into trouble at school for smacking the teacher's bottom.

Try to hold in mind these children as you go through the book.

Sit quietly with your eyes closed for a moment and visualize a child you know with AD/HD. Also note down how you feel about this child. How does the child make you feel when you are in their company? Then open your eyes and quickly jot down as many of their characteristics as possible. Looking at how people make us feel can often help us understand how they are feeling – that puts us in a much better position to be able to help them.

To be successful with a child with AD/HD you need an understanding of what it is like to be a child with AD/HD. You also need some understanding of your own make-up and your response to the child. Some people have a natural ability to empathize with AD/HD children and can get the best out of them – others have to learn how.

The AD/HD-type person finds controlling impulses very difficult and, even when they know something is not desirable behaviour, the part of their brain that works to inhibit impulse just won't seem to work properly. As a consequence impulsive acts are committed and trouble often ensues. In addition to this, concentration can easily waver and omissions of behaviour take place, so not only can the AD/HD child be doing the wrong thing, they omit to do the right thing too.

Attention-deficit hyperactivity disorder (AD/HD) is defined as a medical condition of people who have developmental, behavioural and cognitive difficulties compared to their peers. It is diagnosed using criteria from either the International Classification of Diseases 10, or *The Diagnostic and Statistical Manual of Mental Disorders IV*. Diagnosis has to be made by a clinician, usually a child psychiatrist or paediatrician. As long ago as 1902 a condition that sounds very similar to AD/HD was described in the medical journal, *The Lancet*, by Dr G. F. Still:

the keynote of these qualities is self-gratification . . . without regard to the good of others or to the larger and more remote good of self. Some of these qualities . . . are natural to children at a certain age and to a certain extent: it is their persistence in a degree unusual for the particular age and not responding to the influences of environment which constitutes their abnormality. (p. 1009)

So, for over 100 years the medical profession has been devising a condition to help understand these behaviours. Depending on whom you talk to AD/HD is understood in different ways. The medical model focuses on the biological/neurological/genetic basis of AD/HD, the psychological one on causes attributable to effects of early situations, and the bio-psycho-social is a mixture. AD/HD does not exist as a discrete and tidy disorder. It is more useful to think of AD/HD as an umbrella term for a number of behaviours that any of us are likely to exhibit under stress, but in AD/HD they are pervasive and persistent when compared with the peer group.

The diagnostic criteria

In either of the two following categories six or more of the nine symptoms must have persisted for at least six months to a degree in excess of that normally found in the peer group.

Category 1 – Inattention
- frequently makes careless mistakes in work, does not attend to detail
- frequently has difficulty maintaining attention in work or play
- frequently does not seem to listen even when spoken to directly
- often does not follow instructions/do homework/chores etc. not due to defiance or lack of understanding
- frequently finds organizing tasks difficult

- often tries to avoid tasks requiring sustained mental effort
- frequently without necessary equipment
- is often easily distracted by normal activity going on around him/her
- frequently forgetful

Category 2 – Hyperactivity and impulsiveness

- often fidgets with hands or feet/squirms in seat
- frequently out of seat
- usually finds he/she has to run everywhere, or climb on walls/banks. In adolescence/ adulthood this may manifest itself in restlessness, e.g. leg twitching, finger tapping
- usually 'on the go' or acts as if 'driven by a motor'
- talks excessively
- is noisy at play
- frequently blurts out answers to questions before hearing full question
- finds waiting turn very difficult to the point of making it impossible for parents/carers to tolerate
- will usually butt into conversations or games

Additional requirements

- some of the symptoms were evident before the age of seven
- symptoms are present in two or more settings
- significant impairment in social, academic or occupational functioning is evident
- symptoms are not due to a mental disorder

Based on these criteria three types of AD/HD are identified:

1. combined type
2. predominantly inattentive type
3. predominantly hyperactive-impulsive type

(American Psychiatric Association: *The Diagnostic and Statistical Manual for Mental Disorders*, 4th edn. Washington DC: APA, 2000)

There are three components to AD/HD: sustaining attention and concentration, controlling impulses and controlling motor activity. A diagnosis is only correctly made when there are problems in these areas over and above those found in the peer group and in more than one setting.

AD/HD type behaviour is found in most people at some time. The factors changing such behaviour into AD/HD are persistence, pervasiveness and intensity. It is thought that the root of the problem lies in the inability to inhibit behaviour. So, for example, we might have a fleeting thought, 'I wonder what it would be like to jump out of this 14-storey window'. Before you know it an AD/HD child could have tried this out!

A child born with an AD/HD disposition will attract much negative feedback for his actions. This is understandable because the adults around will have the child's safety in mind. They will also be concerned about social training and the constant effort required to keep the child safe, attended to, on task, etc., is likely to result in fatigue for parents, carers and school staff. Very quickly the child begins to build up a negative self image. This in itself is possibly the most damaging influence on a child's personal and social development. As professionals we should not apportion blame, we should increase our understanding and encourage pupils to adopt good habits. We also need to look after ourselves and preserve our ability to respond appropriately.

Identification and diagnosis of AD/HD is growing at an ever-increasing rate. As school staff look at this significant portion of the population (some estimates say around 5 per cent or one pupil in every class (NICE 2006)) with increased understanding, this means increased life chances for the child, and increased job satisfaction and hopefully less stress for yourself. Everyone benefits.

Some pupils diagnosed with AD/HD will be offered drug therapy. The general consensus of opinion is that drug therapy should be offered as part of a treatment package that includes some behavioural therapy as well. The commonly used drugs are Ritalin (methylphenidate hydrochloride) and Dexedrine (dextroamphetamine). Both are stimulants that increase the effect of neurotransmitters in the brain. It is the ineffectiveness of these neurotransmitters that is thought to be the cause of AD/HD type behaviour.

Activity: What do children with AD/HD look like?

Look at the list below. Put a mark next to any characteristics that you have found in children you have worked with.

1   Noisy – e.g. talking or shouting out of turn in lessons and shouting or banging things when parents are trying to make a phone call   ☐

2   Dreamy   ☐

3   Persistently wandering around the classroom   ☐

4   Irritating classmates/playmates by interfering with them physically, e.g. flicking as they walk by, sticking leg out to trip up   ☐

5   Appearing deaf to instructions   ☐

6   Losing temper quickly – low frustration tolerance   ☐

7   Taking dangerous risks   ☐

8   Butterflying from one task to another   ☐

9   Finding a piece of work difficult to finish   ☐

10 Poor organization of equipment ☐

11 Forgetting to do things ☐

12 Forgetting necessary equipment ☐

13 Excessive demand for attention from all around ☐

14 An inexhaustible amount of energy ☐

15 Fidgets, e.g. taps fingers, twitches leg while sitting, wriggles in seat, sits on feet ☐

16 Deviates from set tasks ☐

17 Difficulty sleeping ☐

18 Difficulty following more than one instruction at a time ☐

19 Giggles while being told off ☐

20 Incessant talking ☐

It is likely that you have put a mark next to more than half of the behaviours above. You are already surprisingly well experienced in working with children with AD/HD-type behaviour. All children exhibit these behaviours some of the time. As stated earlier, the difference is the frequency and intensity that the problem occurs. Sometimes AD/HD occurs without the H part, meaning that children are hypoactive, or very dreamy and find difficulty in getting onto and applying themselves to a task. These children also lack attention and concentration, and many of the strategies useful for the hyperactive form of the condition will be useful for engaging the hypoactive child as well. Often these children – like Ellie and Darren in our virtual group – can be easily missed because they do not exhibit the 'in your face' acting out behaviours that demand attention. The incidence of AD/HD in females is debatably a quarter of that in males. This may be because the associated behaviours

tend to be a little less disruptive in females; also males are more susceptible to any special need as it is considered the male brain is slightly less
able to compensate for difficulties because the communication between
the two hemispheres is not as effective as in the female brain. It seems
that wherever AD/HD is looked for it is found; it is not linked to race.

Intelligence

People with AD/HD tend to be of average to above average
intelligence.

Using diagnostic criteria ICD10 diagnosis for AD/HD will
not be given for a person with an IQ less than 50. Children
with moderate or severe learning disability may exhibit inattentive and hyperactive behaviour in accordance with their
developmental age, but not chronological age – this is not
AD/HD.

To be able to deal best with AD/HD children you need to get
to know their particular strengths and weaknesses. Knowledge
will empower you in helping the pupil with AD/HD.

Girls and AD/HD

There is growing concern regarding the number of girls who
may be AD/HD. The diagnostic criteria for AD/HD are
probably missing out on many girls who actually suffer from
AD/HD, because of their bias towards acting out male-type
behaviour and because the behaviour patterns in boys are
easier to recognize. It may be that there are almost as many
girls you are working with who have undiagnosed AD/HD as
there are boys. For this reason it is a good idea to look at what
an AD/HD girl might look like and consider what you as a TA
can do to help her to succeed in school and later in life. As indicated before, understanding has to be the greatest healer.

The three case studies on Wendy, Ellie and Emma above give
some indication of how girls with AD/HD can appear. As you
can see they can be as varied as the boys. Girls with AD/HD

can go through years of misunderstanding and underachievement. In the teenage years sexual promiscuity can take over as an overriding unsafe behaviour. Often AD/HD women will try to advance on far too many fronts at once. Their houses will be messy. At work their desks are likely to be very untidy and they can get very stressed from an inability to prioritize and organize their tasks. Daily tasks that other people seem to be able to organize easily pose a big problem to the AD/HD woman, often causing her to go into an 'overload' situation resulting in stress and tetchiness with family members. The problems faced by a female AD/HDer are exacerbated by the expectation by society that women nurture, organize the family and keep house. However, there is much that can be done once it is recognized that some women need extra help focusing and organizing themselves, and then their families. AD/HD coaching is growing in popularity right now, and rightly so. Coaching can provide just what a girl or woman needs to help her to get to know herself and be able to use her talents more effectively.

What AD/HD may look like in school

Behavioural inconsistency

One of the most infuriating characteristics of AD/HD for the adults around the AD/HD child is the inconsistency of the behaviour. One minute you can be having an adult level conversation feeling you are really connecting with this child, and the next the child can be bouncing around the classroom like a powerball. AD/HD children can at times perform tasks as well as many others of their peers; they may be able to concentrate on complex tasks for a period of time, but the effort involved can sometimes result in a quick shift in behaviour to something that makes the adult feel personally affronted and downright disheartened. This confusing behaviour can result in judgements being made and unhelpful labels like, naughty, lazy, defiant, being attached to the child. These labels once applied are hard to replace. In our role as education professionals we need to suspend judgement and maintain our own balanced emotional state while working with such challenging children. Because the AD/HD personality thrives on novelty and high stimulation it is possible for good performance and concentration to be observed in unusual situations. This again is particularly irritating for the usual team of adults around the child as a new person can come along and the child will be great for them. However, after a period of time the usual behaviour will return. The process of enabling the child to modify their behaviour takes years of skilful practice and ultimate patience on the part of the adults involved.

Low self-esteem
Anyone who has worked with children with AD/HD will have observed how they often have a real 'downer' on themselves, unable to believe that they are much good at anything. People do seem to have different innate levels of self-esteem, and it appears that AD/HD types are frequently poorly endowed in this area. Couple this with average to above average intelligence and we see an individual who feels very dissatisfied with their performance because they are bright enough to know that they 'should' be doing better. This mismatch of ability and performance/achievement is often only aggravated by schools telling children they have the ability to do something and should be doing better. I look back on myriad times I have been in multidisciplinary meetings with pupils and heard, and even I'm sorry to have to say have said it myself, that 'You could do so much better than you are doing if only you could concentrate . . .'. I can still picture some of the faces, and see the abject despair, the glazed eyes as they switched off from yet another person who had no idea what it was like inside their head.

Executive function deficits

Working memory, memorizing facts, time keeping and getting started on work, self talk and sequencing, controlling emotions, planning for future events are all executive functions which may be developmentally delayed in the AD/HD child.

Working memory capacity is the ability to keep and use information over a short period of time. People who are considered to be 'absent-minded' may have a poor working memory. You have probably experienced working memory problems yourself on occasions; for example, have you ever gone upstairs to look for something and minutes later been asking yourself what it was you went up there for? Or, have you sat in a lecture or talk and been listening when asked to do something, but when it came to doing it you couldn't quite get the instructions sorted in your head and you got confused and switched off from the task? That is your working memory letting you down. AD/HD people can have working memory problems which makes life difficult in areas where sequencing of thoughts and events is needed; for example when trying to plan ahead they may feel overloaded and confused. Some people use lists of things that they need to do, and then work on prioritizing them to good effect. Following a plot in a book may also cause difficulties and make story reading most unenjoyable and even nonsensical. Of course none of this means the AD/HD person will be unable to remember in detail things from the past, or unable to understand and explain complex technicalities, but what it does mean is that in school we need to allow for a poor working memory and introduce techniques that the child will be able to internalize and use as they travel through life, always remembering though that the process of learning these techniques will be slow.

Friendship and social difficulties

Children with AD/HD can find it difficult to make and keep friends. They may be just too much to handle physically, not knowing their own strength or not knowing when to stop doing or saying something. Reading social cues can be very difficult for AD/HD people. Indeed AD/HD adults also suffer from these difficulties. You may know of people who cannot stop talking when it seems so obvious to everyone else that it is time to allow the other person to talk, or to let them get away. Adults are usually a little more tolerant and kinder than children and the AD/HD child is likely to have their self-esteem knocked by other children who don't want to play with them any more.

Poor response to incentives

This means that working to rewards is difficult, and frequently the thought of rewards in the future has very little effect on behaviour. Some success has been gained by using a response cost system where tokens are given at the beginning of a period and taken away when negative behaviour is engaged in. This way the child has something very concrete to see, i.e. rewards disappearing, which seems to work fairly well with many AD/HD children. There appears to be more incentive to defend and maintain what they already have, than to work towards something they may never get.

Learning difficulties

As previously mentioned in the self-esteem section, children with AD/HD frequently appear to be underachieving. Low levels of concentration, a low boredom threshold, a constant desire for new experiences and novelty, frequently resulting in fidgety behaviour, working memory deficits with the resulting sequencing problems, poor organization of self and equipment, all contribute to difficulties in the average classroom. As you read you are likely to be picturing children you work with who exhibit these characteristics. Spelling and handwriting difficulties are also frequently observed in AD/HD children. Some AD/HD children may appear particularly clumsy and dyspraxic.

Testing behaviour

A characteristic of AD/HD is lack of inhibition. Because of this the AD/HD mind finds it difficult to distinguish between those behaviours that are acceptable to engage in and those that should be avoided. Learning the difference can take a lot longer than in the majority of children. As a result it is likely that seemingly outrageous behaviour will be observed, and again the onlooker can be shocked and affronted because the child who is at other times completely reasonable does something completely stupid. Just take a second or two to drift through some thoughts of your own. Have you ever imagined doing something life-threatening or completely outrageous? Now you are likely to be able to screen out those thoughts and refrain from carrying them out, so you wouldn't actually run in front of a bus to find out what it felt like, or jump off a cliff, or out of a high window, or run up to one of your teachers and slap them on the bum, but if you were AD/HD you might! Our task is to walk alongside the child and coach them while they are in the process of gaining some ability to screen and inhibit. The walk can be a long one, but along that walk it has to be remembered that this lack of inhibition has a part to play in the development of the human race. We need risk takers in society, we need people who will challenge existing boundaries and are prepared to engage in testing behaviour. If we look at AD/HD as part of a continuum of personality types we can see that it has a distinct and useful role to play.

Throughout this book at the end of each chapter is a quiz. This is a light-hearted way to help you remember what you have read. At the back you will find the quiz grids reproduced complete with comments. Please go ahead and have a go at the quiz – it's a great way to learn and a method you might like to use in the future.

Review

Quiz

	Yes	No	Maybe

1   A condition like AD/HD was described by medics over 100 years ago ☐ ☐ ☐

2   Almost everyone shows AD/HD type behaviour at times ☐ ☐ ☐

3   Some studies estimate the occurrence of AD/HD is around 25 per cent ☐ ☐ ☐

4   AD/HD is not a medical condition and can be diagnosed by an educational or clinical psychologist ☐ ☐ ☐

5   Not all AD/HD children are hyperactive ☐ ☐ ☐

6   AD/HD is less diagnosed in girls than in boys because the diagnostic criteria are biased towards boyish behaviour patterns ☐ ☐ ☐

7   For AD/HD to be diagnosed the problem behaviours must have been seen before the age of 5 ☐ ☐ ☐

8   Sexual promiscuity in teenage girls can be a sign of AD/HD ☐ ☐ ☐

9   One of the biggest problems for an AD/HD child is lack of understanding of how the AD/HD brain works and a negative attitude shown by society ☐ ☐ ☐

10 All AD/HD children find concentrating difficult at times ☐ ☐ ☐

	Yes	No	Maybe

11 One of the most infuriating characteristics of AD/HD is that one minute you can be having an adult-level conversation and the next the child can be bouncing round the classroom like a powerball ☐ ☐ ☐

12 Children with AD/HD are usually excellent timekeepers and start their work quickly ☐ ☐ ☐

13 Because of social clumsiness children with AD/HD can find it hard to keep friends ☐ ☐ ☐

14 AD/HD has an evolutionary function ☐ ☐ ☐

15 Children with AD/HD are often hypercritical of themselves and have low self-esteem ☐ ☐ ☐

16 Children with AD/HD are usually of below average intelligence ☐ ☐ ☐

17 Some children with AD/HD seem as though they cannot stop talking ☐ ☐ ☐

18 Some children with AD/HD choose to sit quietly at the back of the room and keep out of social interactions ☐ ☐ ☐

19 Children with AD/HD will often engage in boundary-testing behaviour ☐ ☐ ☐

20 For AD/HD to be diagnosed the problem behaviours must have been regularly seen in at least two settings, i.e. home and school ☐ ☐ ☐

2

Why you need to know about AD/HD

This chapter

- outlines why you need to know about AD/HD
- puts AD/HD into the inclusion context
- illustrates other conditions that may mimic AD/HD

Why you need to know about AD/HD

Having read through Chapter 1 you may be thinking that AD/HD is a medical condition and therefore is cared for by the doctor in the child's life. Although AD/HD can only be diagnosed by a doctor, those of us working with children on a day by day basis are under a duty of care to look out for special learning needs, and AD/HD certainly presents a special learning need, as well as requiring specialized parenting. Children with an AD/HD type personality are very likely to experience difficulties in many areas of their life; in fact it is because of these difficulties that they have been taken for medical consultations and diagnosis. The journey for an AD/HDer lasts a lifetime, it doesn't suddenly disappear; it is, as I have suggested previously, a personality type and personality types tend to influence the way we behave for the whole of our lives. In addition more and more children are being diagnosed as having AD/HD-type personalities. In making an accurate diagnosis the clinician needs good information from everyone who knows the child. Sometimes we see children in school who appear to have a misdiagnosis. Being better informed means fewer children will be diagnosed incorrectly and more correctly, resulting in better support.

Your role in school is likely to be quite intensively focused on a small number of children. You may at some time be asked to work with an AD/HD child, very much like some of the children in our virtual group mentioned at the beginning of the book. AD/HD children are very challenging to work with, for reasons that can be very different from the kind of reasons other children are difficult to work with. Often AD/HD children are intelligent and able, but are considered to under-achieve significantly. What needs to be remembered is that academic achievement is reliant on far more than intelligence. One of my oldest friends has done far better in life and aca-demically than other friends who were far more 'intelligent', simply because she had the concentration and determination to stick at her studies. Not everyone has this ability at their finger tips, and it is useful to remember that life is interesting, and the human race has become very innovative, because we are all different, having different skills and gifts which, when put together with other people's, contribute something to society. As educators we need to have a positive eye on the lives of our students 20 years into the future, and realize that there are many different ways of getting an education. In your position as TA you can influence young people by helping them to believe in themselves, and you can influence other staff to believe in them too. Sometimes though, this is really hard to do with AD/HD pupils and you may find you are a lone voice, but have faith, that child will never forget you if you keep believing they can find their niche in life and succeed, and after all that's what everyone wants, isn't it?

Below is a short success story about a boy with AD/HD. The story is taken from a diary written by the boy's mother over a four-year period. The book illustrates very well the problems encountered on a day by day basis when you live with AD/HD, but also illustrates some things do work, and that it is worth persevering.

Stefan

Stefan takes part in a badminton class each week. Tonight I stayed to watch. He was playing with one of the coaches. I was greatly impressed. Stefan had become a very good player, and with his quick reactions could reach some shots that no one else could. He played a game of expertise. This skill has not come about by chance. About three years ago, Stefan went to some children's holiday activities. He disrupted the classes each time he went until the supervisors told me for safety reasons he would not be allowed to go during any other school holidays – the story of our lives.

However, one coach, a lady who ran the badminton part of the activities, saw things in a different light, and was not willing to give up on him and discard him along with the rest. We bless the day we ever met her. She told us to bring Stefan to her sessions and she would take responsibility for him and face the consequences. She saw beyond the problem, she saw a child who had potential and she was determined to do something about it.

She began to teach him the skills on a one-to-one basis. This continued for a long time. Over the months, she gradually introduced first one player, then another and another until Stefan could play with her, in a foursome. It took a lot of time and a lot of patience and skilful handling of situations on her part. She never once gave up on him, She believed in him and learned when to divert his attention when he was becoming bored with one activity. He learned to love this lady and rewarded her efforts by responding to her careful coaching. What a joy it was to watch the result of the past three years and to see how well he played and handled being in a class of people. How much we owe this wonderful lady who has done so much for him, and purely from the kindness of her heart. She is one of those 'one-in-a-million' people!

(Jacky Fletcher, *Marching to a Different Tune – Diary about an AD/HD Boy*. London: Jessica Kingsley, 1999, p. 113)

We all have beliefs and attitudes about what motivates behaviour, and what constitutes good and bad behaviour. Children who have AD/HD look at times indistinguishable from those who do not have AD/HD. As a consequence they can easily be labelled lazy, naughty and slow because of our expectation coupled with their apparent low achievement. They can also be considered defiant and rude. They suffer with both the difficult to control behaviour and the confusion it causes them, plus rejection from peers, and disapproval from teachers, parents and relatives. Such rejection can lead to other mental health problems. I hope that you can see how important you are in the life of the AD/HD child whom you are supporting. You have a crucial role to play, and may from time to time need support yourself in coping with this role. The child mental health charity Young Minds has a telephone helpline called Parents' Information Service, which is available to any adult with a concern about the mental health of a young person. The number is 0800 018 2138.

Inclusion and AD/HD

Inclusion means that more and more children with special needs are being educated in their local school. This puts immense pressure onto schools and means all staff need to be better informed of the vast array of special needs they are likely to be faced with on a day-to-day basis. Your role as TA means you may be in very close contact with these special pupils, and your knowledge will have to be up to meeting the challenge. You are likely to face resistance for some of your ideas from other staff who may not have thought things through in as much detail as you will have done following the reading you are doing right now.

However, there is light at the end of the tunnel because good classroom practice for the AD/HD child is good for all children, so if good practice is employed, everyone benefits. But, is good classroom practice enough? Perhaps we should be thinking in terms of advanced classroom practice with AD/HD children? AD/HD children are very challenging; they are not the only very challenging group of children in schools, but they are possibly a paradoxical group because they often look so bright and able that they trick you into thinking they can achieve more than their nervous system will allow at this stage in its development. Our task is to ensure their self image is kept sufficiently intact so that when the nervous system catches up with their intellect they can get back into the learning zone. If we don't do this we run the risk of mental health issues, disaffection, a life of crime . . . and even sometimes when we do.

There is a legal requirement on schools to enable disabled pupils equal access to the curriculum. The Disability Act 2001 defines disability as 'a physical or mental impairment with an adverse effect on the pupil's ability to carry out normal day to day activities'; the effect must be substantial and long-term (12 months +). AD/HD is considered a disability. Local authorities and schools must not treat disabled pupils less favourably than non-disabled without justification. Local authorities must plan to increase environmental access, curriculum access and access to information for disabled pupils. The Disability Act 2001 may help to encourage more creative solutions to curriculum access, and you in your position of close and exceptional knowledge about particular pupils could be instrumental in creating those solutions. Working with TAs over a number of years in advisory services I have seen some very innovative solutions to children's and families' problems and seen some fantastic work done. As a TA you need to take opportunities to discuss in school different ways of working, and always try to ensure you are at multidisciplinary meetings when the child is discussed: you are in a position to contribute your observations, and they should be first-hand if possible.

Meeting the needs – Maslow's hierarchy of needs

The psychologist Abraham Maslow (1954) proposed that we are all motivated by needs and that our needs are arranged in a hierarchy. At the bottom of the hierarchy are basic physical needs, for example food, water, warmth, shelter, air, sleep. The next level is that of safety and security, health and family. Up a further level he placed love and belonging, friendships and family. It is around this level that we are expecting children to operate in school. On the next level came self-esteem, confidence, achievement, respect of others and respect by others. At the very top is self-actualization where a sense of morality, creativity, spontaneity, problem-solving, lack of prejudice, acceptance of facts are gained.

Maslow's hierarchy of needs states that we must satisfy each need in turn and only when the lower-order needs of physical and emotional well-being are satisfied are we concerned with the higher-order needs of influence and personal development. If the lower-order needs are not met, we are no longer concerned about the maintenance of our higher-order needs. Consequently when we want children to operate at levels three and four of the hierarchy we need to make sure needs at levels one and two are met. The needs requirement differs from child to child, and for the AD/HD child meeting the needs is a bigger challenge. We need to be able to understand the needs of the child if we are to be able to meet them. Getting to know AD/HD children and getting to understand how their brains work is a crucial factor in meeting needs, before learning can take place. This book aims to help you understand AD/HD and so meet the needs more effectively.

Using Maslow's hierarchy of needs we can apply the needs audit below to children we work with to check if we have fulfilled the three lower orders of need before we can consider the child to be in a fit state for learning.

Activity: Needs audit

Choose two children in the class you work with: one you consider performs very well in school and the other an AD/HD child. Apply the needs audit and compare the findings. What does this tell you about what we should be concentrating our efforts on in school to enable learning for these children?

AD/HD child's learning needs audit	Yes	No
Need – Physiological	☐	☐
Has the child had enough to eat today?	☐	☐
Has the child recently had a drink of water?	☐	☐
Has the child had enough sleep in the last 24 hours?	☐	☐
Is the child constipated?	☐	☐
Is the child suffering from any illness that makes him feel generally uncomfortable?	☐	☐
Need – Safety		
Does the child feel safe in school? (Is he scared of anyone, of any situation in school?)	☐	☐
Does the child feel safe within his family? (Is he suffering abuse or neglect? Is the family breaking up?)	☐	☐
Does the child feel happy about the health of his family members? (Is anyone close to him ill at the moment?)	☐	☐
Does the child feel safe about his home? (Are the family about to be evicted?)	☐	☐

Need – Love/belonging	Yes	No
Does the child have a friend in school?	☐	☐
Does the child feel he belongs in his school?	☐	☐
Does the child experience comradeship when he arrives in school?	☐	☐
Does anyone hold him in mind at school so that when he comes in he knows someone has been thinking about him when he was not there?	☐	☐
Does he have anyone in school who has a true under-standing of his needs and works hard to try to meet them?	☐	☐
Does he get the feeling when he has been away that he has been missed for the right reasons – i.e. not because it has been quiet and peaceful while he was away but because his lively/kind/lateral-thinking/problem-solving personality was missed?	☐	☐

(Inspired by Maslow's hierarchy of needs)

Synonyms and mimics

The terminology surrounding AD/HD can be confusing. The terms attention-deficit disorder and attention-deficit hyperactivity disorder (DSM IV) are frequently used synonymously. Hyperkinetic disorder is the term used by the International Classification of Disease: 10, DAMP – deficits in attention, motor and perception – is a Swedish synonym. The definition in the *Diagnostic and Statistical Manual of Mental Disorders* (DSM) has developed over the years.

The table below shows the development of the diagnostic criteria since 1980 to the currently used criteria DSM IV (1994).

	DSM version			
	DSM III (1980)	DSM III R (1987)	DSM IV (1994)	Observed trend
Title	Attention deficit-disorder	Attention-deficit hyperactivity disorder (ADHD)	Attention-deficit/ hyperactivity disorder	Recognition of attention deficit with or without hyperactivity
Essential features	Signs of developmentally inappropriate inattention and impulsivity	Developmentally inappropriate degrees of inattention, impulsiveness, and hyperactivity	Persistent pattern of inattention and/or hyperactivity-impulsivity that is more frequent and severe than typically observed in individuals at a comparable level of development	Consistent emphasis on developmentally inappropriate degrees of inattention, impulsiveness, and hyperactivity
Subtypes	1. Attention-deficit disorder with hyperactivity 2. Attention-deficit	No further clarification on subtypes	1. Attention-deficit/hyper-activity disorder, combined	No significant changes

	DSM III (1980)	DSM III R (1987)	DSM IV (1994)	Observed trend
	disorder without hyperactivity 3. Residual type for those diagnosed with (1) but where hyper-activity is no longer present but other signs persist		type 2. Attention-deficit/ hyperactivity disorder, pre-dominantly inattentive type 3. Attention-deficit/ hyperactivity disorder, pre-dominantly hyperactive-impulsive type	
Forms of disorder	DSM says it is not clear whether or not there are two forms of a single disorder	No further clarification		
Associated features	Vary as a function of age and include obstinacy, stubbornness, negativism, bossiness, bullying,	Vary as a function of age and include mood lability, low frustration tolerance, temper out-bursts, low	Vary depend-ing on age and develop-mental stage, may include low frustra-tion toler-ance, temper outbursts,	

	DSM III (1980)	DSM III R (1987)	DSM IV (1994)	Observed trend
	increased mood lability, low frustration tolerance, temper outbursts, low self-esteem and lack of response to discipline	self-esteem. Academic under-achievement is characteristic	bossiness, stubbornness, excessive and frequent insistence that requests be met, mood lability, demoralization, dysphoria, rejection by peers, and poor self-esteem	
Co-morbidity	Non-localized 'soft' neurological signs and motor-perceptual dysfunctions (poor hand/eye coordination) may be present	Oppositional defiant disorder, conduct disorder and specific developmental disorders are often present. Functional encopresis and functional enuresis are sometimes seen. Non-localized 'soft' neuro-	Oppositional defiant disorder, conduct disorder, mood disorders, anxiety disorders, learning disorders, communication disorders, Tourettes disorder	Consistently associated with oppositional defiant disorder and conduct disorder

	DSM III (1980)	DSM III R (1987)	DSM IV (1994)	Observed trend
		logical signs and motor-perceptual dysfunctions (poor hand/eye coordination) may be present		
Age at onset	Typically by the age of three	Before the age of four	DSM states it is difficult to establish diagnosis before the age of four or five, but does allude to identification at earlier ages (2/3 years)	Recognized age of onset decreasing
Course	Three characteristic courses identified: 1. all symptoms persist into adolescent/ adult life 2. all symptoms	Disorder usually persists throughout childhood. Oppositional defiant disorder or conduct disorder often develop. Conduct disorder often develops into	Parents usually observe signs when child is a toddler. Diagnosis tends to be made in early school years. Tends to be relatively	Tends to be a persistent disorder

	DSM III (1980)	DSM III R (1987)	DSM IV (1994)	Observed trend
	disappear at puberty 3. hyper-activity disappears, but attention and impulsiv-ity difficulties persist (residual type)	antisocial personality disorder in adulthood. Conduct disorder coupled with low IQ and severe mental disorder in parents predicts a poor course	stable throughout adolescence/ adulthood	
Impair-ment	Academic and social. Infrequently residential treatment may be needed	Social and school	Can be very imparing affecting social/school/ familial adjustment	Recognition of familial impairment as well as social/school
Predispos-ing factors	Mild/ moderate mental retardation, epilepsy, some forms of cerebral palsy, and other neurological disorders	Central nervous sytem abnor-malities, i.e. neurotoxins, cerebral palsy, epilepsy, and other neuro-logic disorders. Disorganized/ chaotic environ-ments, child abuse/neglect	Can be very imparing affecting social/school/ familial adjustment	Recognition of familial impairment as well as social/school

	DSM III (1980)	DSM III R (1987)	DSM IV (1994)	Observed trend
Prevalence	Common, 3%	Common, 3%	3%–5%	Increasing rate
Sex ratio	Ten times more common in male than female	Six to nine times more common in males than females	Male to female ratio ranging from 4:1 to 9:1	Recognition of condition in females increasing
Familial pattern	More common in family members than general population	More common in first-degree biologic relatives than general population. Among family members specific developmental disorders, alcohol abuse, conduct disorder and antisocial personality disorder are over-represented	More common in first-degree biologic relatives. Higher prevalence of mood/anxiety disorders, learning disorders, substance-related disorders and antisocial personality disorder in family members.	

(Spohrer 2006)

You will see from the table above that the term AD/HD has developed over the years. There are a number of conditions and situations that produce very similar if not identical behaviour to AD/HD. As stated previously the behaviour needs to be in excess of that of the peer group; however, even within the peer group there will be normal variations, and some children are naturally very boisterous, but may be able to inhibit behaviours when socially necessary, which do not thus constitute a pervasive and impairing condition. Some children may also become very active under certain conditions, for example, just prior to emptying the bowel, agitation can sometimes be observed; also when hungry and blood-sugar levels are a little low; or after sugar has been taken in and blood-sugar levels are high. Also certain foods are regularly suspected of producing behavioural problems in some children. Many artificial colourings are thought to be triggers for hyperactive behaviour, and some children may be dairy or wheat allergic without knowing. Sometimes these children will crave the very foods they are allergic to. Be on the lookout for children who like to eat excessive amounts of dairy or wheat products. Also, other family members having food allergies, eczema and asthma indicate that allergies/intolerances are a possibility. If you do suspect links between behaviour and food try to get the parents/carers to seek a referral through the GP to a nutritionist. It is also useful here to discuss the situation with your school health nurse who may be able to help persuade the parents/carers to seek further help, or be able to give some advice themselves.

In addition to food intolerances, deficiencies in minerals can also be a cause of hyperactivity which can be significantly reduced with dietary management. There has been much in the press over recent years to support the theory that diet and behaviour are linked, but it is still difficult in some areas to get dietary screening before children go onto medication for AD/HD. Reactions to man-made chemicals in foods can be apparent within 15 minutes. Some fruits and vegetables also cause adverse reactions, so it is not just artificial additives that are dietary culprits. Some heavy metals in the diet, for example cadmium, lead and mercury cause a reduction in zinc uptake which reduces the functioning of the neurotransmitters. Some children also have problems absorbing nutrients into the body. This is a massive area and not appropriate for inclusion in any great detail in this book, but for more information go to www.hacsg.org.uk the website for the Hyperactive Children's Support Group which is a mine of excellent information on diet and allergy.

You will no doubt have observed children who seem to be particularly agitated at certain predictable times; there is usually a good reason for this. Some children regularly get more and more excitable or anxious as the weekend approaches; they may be going to stay with a different parent where things are more exciting, or more chaotic, or they may come to school on a Monday with anxiety. All of these factors have behavioural impacts and need observation and some understanding if appropriate support is to be provided.

The environment in the classroom can also have a big effect on activity and concentration levels. For example, children who are very able can be bored in class, and conversely children with a learning difficulty can be anxious; both anxiety and boredom can cause inattentive, hyperactive and disruptive behaviour. Substituting boredom with extra responsibility and challenges, and anxiety with a more secure and emotionally holding environment could pay dividends.

Some medications can also produce behaviour mimicking AD/HD, for example some of the epilepsy drugs. Studies estimate 20 per cent of patients with epilepsy may also present features of AD/HD (Tan and Appleton 2005). In addition hypoglycaemic diabetes can be mistaken for AD/HD. Again a significant proportion of children with diabetes are also thought to have AD/HD. Monitoring of medication is a very important task in a good support package. Later in the book you will find samples of medication monitoring sheets that you may like to adapt for your own use in school.

Sleep difficulties

Sleep apnoea is a condition in which a person stops breathing for a very short time every few minutes during sleep due to their airway being blocked by their tongue and throat. Children with mild hyperactive behaviour may have this condition. AD/HD children often find sleep elusive; lack of sleep and consequential irritability due to tiredness is likely to affect behaviour in the classroom. Again, before a diagnosis is made, a sleep pattern investigation is advised.

Sensory modulation/sensory integration dysfunctions

Sensory modulation or sensory integration is the neurological process by which we receive information from our senses and filter it for use. Children with specific developmental difficulties of poor motor and behavioural organization are thought by some researchers not to sense the world in the way most others do. Their bodies and brains use the sensations they are receiving in a way that creates disorganization and excessive motor activity. These problems are considered to take place way inside the brain without any conscious control. The theory of sensory integration was suggested by Dr Jean Ayres, an occupational therapist who observed children with the specific difficulties outlined above, and found that by directing and controlling the input of different senses, improvements in learning and organization were gained. It is possible that some children exhibiting AD/HD-type behaviour have a sensory dysfunction, and may thus be seeking or avoiding certain stimulation which results in behavioural difficulties. Understanding what the stimuli are that are needed more and less will help in the classroom, and to do this it is necessary to calibrate on the child's behaviour and to remember Maslow's hierarchy of needs – we all need certain basic needs met before we are in a fit state for learning; if our needs are quite a bit different from many others in our class it's likely they won't be met as often and as easily and we will misbehave relative to our peers.

Central auditory processing disorder (CAPD)

Many of the behaviours exhibited by CAPD children are identical to AD/HD. For example: easily distracted, difficulty following instructions, difficulty with with reading, spelling, writing; with comprehending abstract information; disorganized and forgetful. CAPDs are not deaf, they just do not process what they hear. They may process only part of what they hear but lose the whole meaning, or they may perceive a totally incorrect idea of what has been said. It is possible to have both CAPD and AD/HD, in fact it is so hard to distinguish one from the other in some cases that it has been said that the diagnosis a child receives can depend on which route he took in getting to the diagnosis, i.e. if he went through the hearing route he is more likely to get a CAPD diagnosis. Clearly medication for AD/HD is unlikely to be the best treatment strategy for a child with CAPD, so accurate diagnosis and support is desirable.

Disorganized/disorientated attachment

Also sometimes known as reactive attachment disorder, this can easily be confused with AD/HD. A child with this type of attachment may be constantly overwhelmed with fear and anxiety and feel helpless in situations where there is no secure emotional or physical base. They tend to cope with this helplessness by taking control of situations, are hyper-vigilant and ready to down tools and go into flight or fight mode, and lack empathy with others (Geddes 2006). It is easy to see how the agitation and hyperactivity of these children can be described as AD/HD. Medication of such a child could mask symptoms and result in inadequate support. This type of attachment is a serious problem and left unsupported will inhibit learning and formation of relationships and is likely to lead onto lifelong problems.

Reactive attachment disorder is caused during a critical period in a child's development – from conception to about two years. During this time if a child suffers from any of the following: maternal ambivalence to pregnancy; sudden separation from the primary care giver; abuse – sexual, physical or emotional; frequent house moves; traumatic prenatal experience; *in utero* exposure to alcohol or drugs; neglect; genetic predisposition; birth trauma; unprepared and inadequate parenting; undiagnosed or painful illness, reactive attachment disorder can ensue. It is worth noting here that the demands made by the AD/HD child are such that the primary caregiver is likely to find parenting so difficult that they will fall into the dubious category of unprepared and inadequate parenting. If this is so then the condition of AD/HD could usefully be added to the list of *causes* of Reactive Attachment Disorder. Many of the behaviours associated with attachment disorders mimic AD/HD so well it is very hard to tell the difference without continued observation of the child and family.

Sensory deficits

Sometimes the lack of attention a child shows is quite simply because their hearing or vision is impaired. Fluctuating hearing loss due to glue ear or loss of hearing in one side can cause children to continually turn the good ear towards the speaker, thus making eye contact difficult, and possibly giving a message of lack of attention. High frequency hearing loss can also cause difficulties as much sense of a sentence can be lost when many of the consonant sounds are misheard. Children can become good at guessing from the context, but will get very obvious things wrong and can look as though they were not listening. Before any diagnosis of AD/HD is made a hearing test should be carried out; these can easily be arranged through the school health nurse, and it is important to say why you think a test is necessary.

Similarly, uncorrected vision difficulties can encourage children to wander around to get a closer look at information they think they need to do the task.

Other disorders

Studies have indicated that closed head injury produces AD/HD behaviour in a significant number of cases (Gerring *et al.* 1998: p. 654). Mild learning difficulties/severe learning difficulties (MLD/SLD), fragile X syndrome, foetal alcohol syndrome, dyslexia, anxiety, receptive language disorder and autism can all present AD/HD-type behaviour.

Response to maternal depression

Depressed mothers are likely to rate their child's behaviour more negatively than non-depressed (Modell *et al.* 2001, Baumann *et al.* 2004). This does not necessarily mean that the views of such mothers should be discarded; on the contrary, it is possible that the innate difficult behaviour of an AD/HD baby/child has contributed to maternal depression and feelings of inability to cope. Neither does it mean that the mother's depression has caused the AD/HD. However, it is another factor to be considered in the diagnostic process, and another reason not to rely on one source of information on a child's behaviour. If the mother is depressed, a different support mechanism is needed for the family/mother/child.

This list of AD/HD mimics is by no means complete, but I hope it does go some way to indicate that we need to explore many possibilities as causes of AD/HD-type behaviour, and that in doing so we can find better ways to support people, and get better outcomes for children, families and schools. With greater understanding everyone benefits. Our aim should always be to create a useful support package regardless of what we call the behaviour patterns we are working with. The more informed you can be of slight differences in conditions the better. Knowledge empowers you to aid in the most effective way. Always keep your mind open for more learning.

> Behaviour is seen as a problem when we wish to control it, it stops being a problem and becomes a resource when we try to understand it.
>
> (BEST development programme – Task Learning Set 4 – Young Minds, Grubb Institute, DfES)

Children with AD/HD will engage in a variety of behaviours that help them to cope with life. Many of these are counter-productive and in fact result in more negative feedback from the adults around them. However, if we can recognize the behaviours for what they are – ways of coping – we can do something about coaching the child in different, more appropriate ways of coping. Examples of coping behaviours that particularly affect work in school include: giving up on tasks; avoiding tasks altogether; avoiding school/truancy/skipping lessons; negative responses to praise, sometimes accompanied by even worse behaviour following praise; class clowning; cheating; avoidance of homework. Out in the playground other coping strategies may be employed to deal with the difficult social situations faced in unstructured times in school, for example: fighting; cheating at games; controlling bullying behaviour; general impulsiveness. At home, as well as many of the other strategies mentioned above, the child may suffer from TV or computer game addiction. This is again an attempt to cope with the need for extra stimulation before the brain can feel satiated and calm. A child may also lie in an effort to cover up his undesirable behaviour, out of wishful thinking or denial, often believing himself in the lie. He may also rationalize his actions very eloquently.

If all of these behaviours are seen as a communication difficulty and something that can be discussed from a perspective of understanding rather than blame, work can be done to coach the child into more appropriate ways of responding. As a coach whenever we see an inappropriate behaviour it is important to try to work out what purpose that behaviour has, and to find another behaviour to substitute which will fulfil a similar need. A good way to do this is encourage the child to write about themselves and their behaviour. An example of this can be found in My Success Book later in this book.

Review

Quiz

		Yes	No	Maybe
1	Some medications and foods trigger AD/HD-type behaviour	☐	☐	☐
2	We should look out for foods children crave as indicators of what they could be allergic to	☐	☐	☐
3	Stress in the classroom never causes AD/HD-type behaviour	☐	☐	☐
4	Attachment disorders can easily be confused with AD/HD	☐	☐	☐
5	AD/HD is managed completely by medics and we as educationalists can have no input into its management	☐	☐	☐
6	AD/HD is a childhood condition that young people grow out of by the time they are 18	☐	☐	☐
7	Working with AD/HD children requires much understanding, patience and perseverance	☐	☐	☐

8   For a child to be able to learn they need their physiological, safety, love/belonging needs to be met first

9   Sometimes ADHD, AD/HD and ADD are used to mean the same thing

10   Diabetes cannot be mistaken for AD/HD

11   Good classroom practice for AD/HD children will not benefit other children in the class

12   Some children's bodies and brains use sensations they are receiving in a way that creates disorganization and excessive motor activity

13   Cheating, lying and giving up easily on work can be seen as AD/HD-coping behaviours

14   When we want a child to change a behaviour we need to help them find something they can replace it with

15   If we understand what sensory stimuli are needed to help a child learn we can aid their learning more effectively

16   The Disability Act 2001 applies to AD/HD

17   As a TA you are in a fantastic position to help young people believe in their own ability to succeed

3

Causes of AD/HD

This chapter:

- looks at the causes of AD/HD
- describes some of the learning difficulties with AD/HD
- suggests some useful strategies

Causes of AD/HD

The precise cause of AD/HD is still being debated, but it is widely agreed that it is a neurological condition affecting the psychological process for attention and inhibition control. There is more and more evidence to show that AD/HD is a genetically based condition, because parents and siblings of children with AD/HD have a higher than expected rate of also being AD/HD. It is thought that a number of defective genes acting together cause the outward signs of AD/HD. It can be a number of different genes acting together. These genes affect the way the neurotransmitters dopamine and norapinephrine are taken up at the synapse between nerves. The additive effect of a number of defective genes cannot be adequately compensated for by other steps in the neurotransmitter metabolism, hence the lack of attention and inhibition seen in AD/HD children. Where AD/HD occurs in a family for what appears to be the first time it is likely that there are a small number of defective genes on each side which previously have never reached the threshold required to become behaviourally evident, but in this genetic mix are in sufficient numbers to show up behaviourally.

AD/HD is far more commonly diagnosed in males than in females because the male brain tends to be less able to compensate for the effect of the defective genes, so it is possible that the required number of defective genes is lower in males than in females. Female brains tend to be better than males at sharing functions between the two frontal lobes of the brain. This is also the case for many other learning difficulties like autism and dyslexia for example.

Thus the genetic mix of the child gives the child a bigger tendency toward AD/HD-type behaviour. This does not mean that the situation is a lost cause; far from it, much can be done to bring out the best from the AD/HD personality, and always remember every coin has two sides. Some aspects of AD/HD behaviour are very useful tools for our society. During puberty the frontal cortex of the brain matures and adolescents become more able to reason and think in an abstract and reflective way. Together with this development comes better impulse control. This frontal lobe 'synaptogenesis' takes place at about 12 years old. At this time the brain is remoulding. You have more than likely unconsciously experienced this change taking place in children you have observed, be they your own children, friends', relatives' or children you work with. You will have noticed how the child changes into a more 'adult' thinker. During this time of synaptogenesis there is a new opportunity for embedding behaviour patterns that may have been impossible to embed before, for whatever reason. If, during this time, the child is in an environment that encourages him to keep on task, reflect on his emotions, exercise self-control, plan for future events, but which does not expect so much that he consistently fails, he is likely to keep hold of some good behaviour patterns and utilize them into adulthood. Medication at this time can be used to help provide a window within which to work.

A question often posed is 'How much of AD/HD behaviour is learned behaviour?' Because of the significant genetic factor it is easy to fall into the trap of assuming behaviour is learned from parents who may exhibit similar traits, but it is important not to forget that the genetic make-up of the child will have a significant bearing on how susceptible to learning certain types of behaviour he/she is. The truth is probably that the behaviour observed is a result of an interaction of biological (genetic) and environmental factors. If you have ever been in the position to be able to observe a child brought up without the influence of a certain older family member, possibly due to bereavement or separation, you will almost certainly have noticed mannerisms and characteristics that have not been learned, but have been passed on through the genes.

AD/HD as a personality type with an evolutionary purpose

Thom Hartmann in his book *Attention Deficit Disorder – A Different Perception* (1999) splits the population into two types, hunters and farmers. He considers that the AD/HD people among us are the hunter types who are quick to respond in emergencies and constantly scanning the environment. The farmers on the other hand are more interested in working towards long-term goals and nurturing situations. Little wonder that females with AD/HD find life so difficult when so much of the female role in society is about long-term nurture.

It is possible that modern-day society exacerbates the negative aspects of the AD/HD personality. The 'hunter' type come into their own when the society within which they live is threatened. In survival mode the skills of the hunter are of use to the whole tribe. Currently though, society is complacent, we have relatively easy lives, we are not at constant risk for survival, it's easy to keep warm and fed, the basic Maslowian needs are easily met. However, should this change, and with global warming, peak oil and political instability in certain parts of the world, the comfort and complacency currently enjoyed by the vast population in the western world, as well as increasingly in the east, may come to a sharp end. Could it be that at that time the AD/HD type personality with its ability to think quickly and laterally and to switch on in a crisis, and act quickly, will come of age?

It is possible that the AD/HD brain works at its best when there is a crisis/survival situation at hand. When the unconscious mind can take over, gut reactions can be followed, when there is no time for conscious thinking about pros and cons of actions the brain is working on an automatic higher plane. There are very few opportunities normally for this kind of brain workout. This could be why crime is attractive to some AD/HD brains, because it creates a need to survive against the enemy and a need for snap decision and action – something that stimulates the AD/HD brain into clear thinking.

What can be done for learning difficulties commonly found with AD/HD children

AD/HD children are invariably considered to underachieve in school. Frequently AD/HD children are of average to above average intelligence and as a consequence teacher expectation can be in line with the IQ rather than the neurological level of development or the EQ – emotional level of intelligence. Mention has been made before of the problems experienced by some AD/HD children when trying to sequence events, tell stories, hold instructions in mind. They are considered to have poor executive functioning so these tasks that come relatively easily to other pupils of the same intellectual ability, may be very hard for the AD/HD child, and may make them look lazy, stupid or obstinate.

Poor concentration
One of the commonest features of AD/HD is poor concentration. Children will be easily distracted in the classroom, preferring to pay attention to each and every noise and motion that happens outside the room or, at the very least, to anything

that isn't what the teacher wants the child to pay attention to! This can be infuriating for the teacher, and you in your role as TA will no doubt have observed interactions between teacher and child just like this. You have probably had them yourself too. It is possibly worth remembering here how the AD/HD brain seems to work. Because of a lack of effectiveness of the neurotransmitters the AD/HD brain is always looking for a top-up of stimulation to feel satisfied and able to rest. As a consequence it gets very easily bored and to avoid boredom and sleep will engage in these diversionary activities. The problem only increases as the level of work required becomes more complex as the child ages.

So, what can you do to help a child with poor concentration?
The first place to start is to look for situations in which the best concentration is gained. Take particular note of how the child feels. Get to know the sensory signs the child gives out when he is able to work and focus, calibrate on the child's behaviour, and work on building rapport. By building excellent rapport you become better able to lead the child into the type of behaviour you require. It is important to ask people to do things when they are in the right sensory state to be receptive to your request. The principles I am describing here are found in Neuro Linguistic Programming. If you can attend a training day or better still a couple of days on NLP for schools do so. You will find it invaluable in being able to connect with your pupils. If you want to find out more about NLP and its applications in the educational context look at www.katespohrer.org.uk.

It may also be that the child is especially sensory sensitive and may need a period of time engaging in a different kind of activity that satisfies a sensory need before he is able to settle and concentrate. For more on sensory integration and how to work out what helps see Chapter 5.

Working memory

Working memory stores instructions on a short-term basis, a little bit like a desk top. However if the desk top gets muddled and cluttered we all know how difficult it is to work clearly and sequentially. When reading a story the working memory can let you down by not holding the last bit of the story, so piecing a story together and making sense of it becomes increasingly difficult. You quite literally 'lose the plot'; once this happens the story stops making any sense and boredom, confusion and anxiety take over. Picture yourself in a classroom where it looks as if everyone else is following the story, but you have just lost the plot. How would you feel in this situation? Happy, confident and comfortable with the situation? We need children to feel all of these to be able to learn; remember Maslow? If they don't, then we are going to find it an increasingly uphill struggle to enable them to learn.

To help a child with working memory problems think about ways to aid the memory. A whiteboard close at hand to put lists on, and to aid in sequencing of tasks can be very useful. There is also something very satisfying and concrete about taking a sponge and wiping away tasks that have been completed. This can give a great sense of achievement, and success begets success.

Lists are also useful to help check if all equipment for a task is in place. The natural tendency of the AD/HD brain could be to see what is around and improvise tools and equipment, not to carry it all with you. Being prepared in this way goes against the grain, but with training the best of both worlds can be achieved. What has to be remembered here is that everyone has differing potentials for achievement, and organization is part of that. Some people function extremely well in the world of work because they have other people doing the administrative and organizational tasks for them. Working together as a team and taking your place in society is what we should keep our eye on as a child grows. We need to help them to make the right choice about the kind of work they go into, for example I would not advise an AD/HD child to aim to become a librarian, but an AD/HD child may well make a great success out of a career in the SAS or as a paramedic, if they can get through the minefield of negativity that surrounds them as they go through childhood and adolescence.

Tony Buzan in his book *Mind Maps for Kids* (2003) recommends using mind maps to retain information. By drawing out a mind map you have a visual reminder in your head of the thing you want to be able to remember. It might be useful to encourage AD/HD children to note stuff down as it is being said to them in the form of a mind map. Often AD/HD children will like to doodle and if they can be directed to doodle in the form of a mind map it could serve a double purpose of extra stimulation so they are satiated and enable them to remember the instructions or the task that they are being expected to do. They may be able to leap-frog stages in the planning process by getting straight into the mind map while they are being told what to do. Remember these children often have very agile minds; it is our task to help them use that agility. If you can train an AD/HD child to use mind maps early in life it could be the tool they need to help with their organization. Remember though that no single strategy will work for everyone, and that no strategy will work every time for an AD/HD child, but this one is certainly worth a try. Remember also that the strategies that work personally for ourselves may not work for the children we work with, but that their strategies could be just as valid, and in fact we could learn new strategies from them. All human beings have an innate desire to make sense of the world and will be working out their own strategies to do this. Some will be better than others, but young people can come up with fresh and effective ideas. Look out for them.

Handwriting

AD/HD children have to work extremely hard on their handwriting to overcome lagging manipulation skills. Handwriting is a very important skill even in this day and age of keyboards. Handwriting can be the first impression you make on another person long before you meet them in person. Using exercises that don't seem related to handwriting, but in fact increase strength and manual dexterity can be a good way to keep the AD/HD child interested in the task. Therapeutic putty, which comes in four strengths of resistance, can be used like plasticine, but with much greater effect as it has the benefit of the different strengths, is far more plastic and lasts a lot longer. Regular use can improve manipulation of pencil and other tools, thus giving the child a greater chance of improving handwriting (for suppliers, see Useful websites). Other exercises illustrated below, like drawing a metre diameter circle on a whiteboard, and filling in as close as possible to the last circle – another circle and another and another, ensuring each time that the pen remains in contact with the board for the whole of each circle.

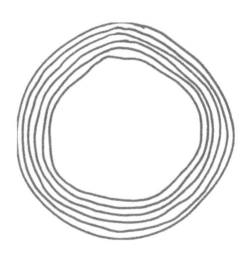

This can be done on a smaller scale on paper too, but on a large board can be a group activity with children taking turns to come up to the board and fill in the circle. This activity is particularly good for concentration and manipulation skills. One of the most intriguing aids to handwriting I have seen is the practice of 'form drawing' found in the Waldorf schools. Form drawing involves the drawing of many shapes and patterns which lead on to good hand/eye coordination skills. Rudolf Steiner, the founder of Waldorf education, believed that the whole human being takes part when drawing a circle, even the eyes make a circular movement; this thinking is echoed in the principles of *Brain Gym* (Dennison and Dennison 1994). An exercise I like to use involves starting with a circle, but this time filling in with a spiral, first in a clockwise direction, then anticlockwise which is derived from form drawing and art therapy, the circular boundary giving containment and harmony to the exercise. These exercises can be done with both dominant and non-dominant hands, helping both sides of the brain to work together. Another harmonizing movement is the figure of eight, also widely used in *Brain Gym*, but found too in the instructions for form drawing (Niederhauser and Frohlich 1984: 8) this time the figure of eight is filled in in a spiralling fashion. Much can be achieved without any actual practice of writing as such. For more information on form drawing see *Form Drawing* by Niederhauser and Frohlich.

Difficulty adhering to rules

The defiant and oppositional behaviour that can accompany AD/HD in the primary years can easily turn into the more serious Oppositional Defiant Disorder (ODD), or the even more serious Conduct Disorder. The diagnostic criteria for ODD cites negative, hostile and defiant behaviour evident for at least six months, causing impairment in social and academic functioning, during which at least four of the following behaviours are evident in excess of that normally found in the peer group:

1 often loses temper
2 often argues with adults
3 often actively defies or refuses to comply with adult requests or rules
4 often deliberately annoys people
5 often blames others for mistakes or misbehaviour
6 is often touchy or easily annoyed by others
7 is often angry and resentful
8 is often spiteful and vindictive

In addition, the behaviour can occur even when the child is not depressed.

The difference between ODD and AD/HD is that the behaviour of ODD is wilful, but the behaviour associated with AD/HD is not generally deliberate and wilful. This is clearly a difficult judgement to make. ODD behaviour can quickly become habitual and very difficult to alter, with a distinct possibility of developing into Conduct Disorder, a more severe behavioural disorder than ODD.

Diagnostic criteria for conduct disorder (CD)

DSM IV (APA 1994) says CD is characterized by persistent and repetitive behaviour where the rights of others or age-appropriate norms are transgressed. These behaviours include:

1 aggressive harmful behaviour
2 non-aggressive behaviour causing harm or loss to property
3 theft or deception
4 serious violation of rules

The criteria require at least three specific symptoms to have occurred in the 12 months prior to diagnosis, with at least one in the preceding six months. Behaviour must also significantly impair social and academic functioning. The criteria should only be able to be met where there is persistent antisocial behaviour as opposed to a single antisocial act.

Young people with conduct disorder show little or no empathy or remorse, and can react with unreasonable hostility to the attention of others. CD is a serious mental health issue, which can indicate a likelihood of developing into early sexual behaviour, substance abuse or self-harming behaviour. Such young people will also be likely truants, high risk takers and have low self-esteem. You can see that some of the characteristics of AD/HD could easily be muddled with CD; however, the difference seems, like ODD, to be the wilfulness of the behaviour, with added severity. The diagnostic criteria, however, are completely different, so it is important to know the criteria for all three conditions as it could be easy to consider a child with CD or ODD to be AD/HD if you did not realize there were such conditions. This might all sound a bit muddling, but it is better to know of the conditions, so more appropriate support can be put in place, and possibly even more importantly, so that the expectations of the adults around the child can be more realistic and understanding. Straight AD/HD should not involve outright wilful and deliberate law-breaking activity on a regular basis, but most children diagnosed ODD or CD will also fulfil the criteria for AD/HD.

Chapter 5 examines the kind of factors that maximize the development of AD/HD in a child, and the factors that can minimize the impact of the condition. Many children with a diagnosis of AD/HD are likely to go on to develop ODD and CD. This is not surprising considering the amount of negative behaviour-specific feedback they get, and if we agree with the theory that the behaviour you want to see more of you give attention to, we, as adults, are creating rods for our own backs when we keep pointing out to a child the behaviour we do not wish to see repeated, because children, like adults, enjoy attention, be it for good or bad.

Review

Quiz

		Yes	No	Maybe

1 AD/HD is thought to be a genetically based condition ☐ ☐ ☐

2 AD/HD is more commonly diagnosed in males than females ☐ ☐ ☐

3 Synaptogenesis is a process in the brain of remoulding which takes place at about 11/12 years. It is an opportunity to instil new patterns of behaviour ☐ ☐ ☐

4 A child with working memory problems can find life easier by using a whiteboard to write lists and aid memory ☐ ☐ ☐

5 AD/HD observed behaviour is a result of an interaction of biological and environmental influences. It is neither all learned nor all inherited ☐ ☐ ☐

6 One gene is responsible for AD/HD ☐ ☐ ☐

7 Mind maps can be a way to switch an AD/HD child onto planning topics ☐ ☐ ☐

8 AD/HD can be tested for with a simple blood test ☐ ☐ ☐

9 Females are better at sharing functions between the two frontal lobes of the brain ☐ ☐ ☐

10 An environment that encourages the child to remain attentive, reflect on thoughts, ☐ ☐ ☐

	Yes	No	Maybe

feelings and emotions, exercise self-control
and plan ahead will have a positive impact
on future behaviour

11 To aid a child's concentration you need to
    look for situations in which the best concen-
    tration is gained and reproduce these as
    much as possible

12 By calibrating on a child's behaviour you
    can build up good rapport and lead a child
    into better behaviour patterns

13 Assessing when a child is in a receptive state
    and choosing times to make requests to do
    unpopular tasks are helpful strategies to
    learn

14 Some children need time engaging in
    certain sensory activities before they are in
    the receptive state

15 The genes responsible for AD/HD affect the
    way neurotransmitters dopamine and
    norapinephrine are taken up at the synapse
    between nerves

16 The male brain is better able to compensate
    for the effect of defective genes

17 Handwriting can only be improved by pure
    handwriting practice

18 If a child has AD/HD they will not have
    Oppositional Defiant Disorder or Conduct
    Disorder

4

Diagnosis

This chapter looks at:

- how AD/HD is diagnosed
- medication
- medication monitoring
- the vice or virtue of the label

Diagnosis

The diagnostic criteria for AD/HD are contained in *The Diagnostic and Statistical Manual of Mental Disorders* (DSM IV 1994). Reference may also be made to The World Health Organization's International Classification of Diseases (ICD 10) where the term Hyperkinetic Syndrome is used. AD/HD can only be diagnosed by a clinician, usually a child psychiatrist or paediatrician. However, AD/HD-type behaviour can be identified by any of us. Identification of AD/HD needs to establish evidence of early age of onset and persistence apparent across a minimum of two settings.

Key factors of AD/HD

- AD/HD is a lifelong condition even though it can modify in adulthood
- it is evident before the age of seven
- it has a biological basis
- it can respond to certain types of medication

- it has a high level of intensity that has an adverse effect on the child's social and cognitive functioning
- it is best diagnosed in early childhood

How is it diagnosed?

A doctor will take information from people who know the child well, for example parents and teachers. Ideally the doctor should be gathering information from several sources that indicate what the child is like in different situations and with different people. AD/HD is a pervasive condition, in other words it should be apparent in most situations the child is in. If it only comes on at school, or at home, it is necessary to look at the environment and see if there are any factors that are increasing the child's anxiety and bringing out AD/HD-type behaviour in specific situations. A diagnosis made only on the comments of school or parent is questionable, and you can probably think of children you know who have a diagnosis, but who are no trouble in school, conversely there may be other children you know, who are a lot of trouble in school, but parents report they are golden at home. What do you think this indicates?

The doctor should also observe and interview the child. Reference will be made to DSM IV as outlined in Chapter 1 and/or the International Classification of Diseases (ICD) 10 and if the criteria are matched sufficiently a positive diagnosis is likely.

How important are you in the diagnosis?

Very! As stated earlier, a good diagnosis will be based upon reports from people who spend a lot of time with the child and know the child well. You are likely be in closer contact with the child than most other adults. Also because you are working with other children and will have made observations you are in a good position to be able to tell what is developmentally appropriate at certain ages. Your observations are very important, but it is also important for you to know what to look out for. You have already heard about some of the mimicking conditions, so you are in a good position to be able to shed light on what problems the child may be facing, and make a great contribution to an adequate support package; and after all that is what we are all working towards, isn't it?

What happens after diagnosis?

Medication

Frequently after diagnosis medication will be offered. In 2004 £13 million was spent in the UK on drugs for AD/HD (NICE, *Review of Technology* Appraisal 98, 2006). There is still controversy over the medication of AD/HD. The generally accepted medical position is that a well-managed medication programme is better than behavioural programmes (The MTA Cooperative Group 1999). This study also suggested combined treatments are no better than medication alone. However, another analysis of research indicated that combined medication and intensive behavioural treatment was better than medication alone (Pritchard 2006). It is probably fair to say that each case needs to be viewed very much on its individual characteristics. We have already seen that AD/HD is in truth an extremely difficult condition to diagnose accurately because it shares many symptoms with other conditions, and is very easy to confuse with them. Because of this it is reasonable to say that no one case of AD/HD will be exactly the same as the next, and neither should be the support package. Treating AD/HD is to some extent a game of hit and miss, that is why constant vigilance on the part of the carers is necessary. Small sensory alterations could give big clues as to what works well for a child and what doesn't. This again is where you are in an important position – to make those observations.

So how does stimulant medication work?
At this point you might want to know a little bit about how a *stimulant* actually works in calming someone down.

Paradoxically Ritalin (methylphenidate hydrochloride) and Dexedrine (dextroamphetamine) are stimulants which increase the effect of neurotransmitters in the brain. It is the ineffectiveness of such neurotransmitters that is thought to be the cause of AD/HD-type behaviour. The AD/HD brain is constantly looking for a sufficient level of stimulation to feel satisfied. Because of the decreased effect of the neurotransmitters it doesn't normally feel satiated. Imagine the brain to be the stomach feeling hungry, then the AD/HD brain feels constantly hungry and is looking for food to take that hunger away. When it is 'fed' by a stimulus, brain activity increases and feels satisfied for a short time. The medication helps the brain to feel well fed.

Despite the ongoing debate, good practice would indicate medication should only be used as part of a multimodal management programme. Medication should be looked on as a short-term strategy with regular checks to ensure its continued effectiveness. Drug treatment holidays for the psychostimulants methylphenidate and dextroamphetamine are still recommended by NICE (2006). Both methylphenidate and dextroamphetamine are central nervous system stimulants which increase the effect of neurotransmitters in the brain.

Assuming then that medication has been offered to a child you are working with, you are likely to want to know a little bit about how it works, and how you can work with the child to capitalize on the effects of the medication. Below is a table that illustrates how some of the more commonly used medications work.

Some advantages of stimulant medication
Medication can have dramatic positive effect in the classroom and at home, improving academic productivity and accuracy, short-term memory, concentration, interaction with parents, teachers and peers.

In addition it can enable social functioning to a level of appropriateness never before achieved by reducing aggression,

Medication	Action
Methylphenidate (Ritalin)	Blocks dopamine transporter 30 minutes to peak effect time. Wears off after 4 hours Slow-release versions of Concerta and Equasym even this out and can last all day
Dextroamphetamine	Releases dopamine from storage vessels Effect wears off after 6 hours
Imipramine (Tofranil)	Inhibits re-uptake of norepinephrine 2/3 weeks' effect time
Clonidine (Catapres)	Blocks norepinephrine autoreceptors Sometimes favoured if child suffers tics
Atomoxetine (Strattera)	Inhibits re-uptake of norepinephrine
Moclobemide (Aurorix)	Inhibits breakdown of dopamine and nor-epinephrine by monoamine oxidase
Fluoxetine (Prozac)	Selective serotonin re-uptake inhibitors (SSRIs) 2/3 weeks' effect time

negative and disruptive behaviour in the classroom and playground, thus giving the child a taste of success on which to build good behaviour habits and better social standing.

Side effects of stimulant medication
Common side effects are loss of appetite, weight loss and sleeplessness. Less frequent ones include: nervousness, mood swings, emotionality, tears, exaggeration of existent tics, anxiety, headaches, hallucinations and initial bruising.

Monitoring medication

It is important to note any observed side effects. The forms below can be adapted and used to aid this process. Once completed they can form a valuable tool for the clinician deciding on appropriate dosage.

Teachers' Monitoring Sheet for a Pupil with AD/HD

Name _____

School _____ Date _____

Age _____ Covering period from _____ to _____

How would you describe the child's self-esteem?

_____

_____

_____

_____

How would you describe the child's interaction with peers?

_____

_____

_____

_____

Please complete the observation sheet below

Observation	Never	Occasion-ally	Often
Makes careless mistakes in work, does not attend to detail	☐	☐	☐
Butterflies from one task to another	☐	☐	☐
Does not seem to listen even when spoken to directly	☐	☐	☐
Does not follow instructions, not due to defiance or lack of understanding	☐	☐	☐
Finds organizing tasks difficult	☐	☐	☐
Tries to avoid tasks requiring sustained mental effort	☐	☐	☐
Loses/without necessary equipment	☐	☐	☐
Easily distracted by normal activity going on around him/her	☐	☐	☐
Forgetful	☐	☐	☐
TOTALS	☐	☐	☐

Hyperactivity and Impulsiveness

	Never	Occasion-ally	Often
Fidgets with hands or feet/squirms in seat	☐	☐	☐
Out of seat	☐	☐	☐
Runs everywhere/climbs on walls (older students may show restlessness, leg twitching, finger tapping)	☐	☐	☐

Diagnosis

	Never	Occasion-ally	Often
Noisy at play	☐	☐	☐
'On the go', acts as if 'driven by a motor'	☐	☐	☐
Talks excessively	☐	☐	☐
Blurts out answer to questions before hearing full question	☐	☐	☐
Finds waiting turn difficult to the point of making it impossible for parents/carers to tolerate. Butts into conversations or games	☐	☐	☐
TOTALS	☐	☐	☐
Demands must be met immediately – easily frustrated	☐	☐	☐
Excessive drowsiness	☐	☐	☐
Withdrawn	☐	☐	☐
Headaches	☐	☐	☐
Motor/vocal tic	☐	☐	☐
Insomnia	☐	☐	☐
Excessive crying/emotionality	☐	☐	☐
Anxiety	☐	☐	☐
Nausea	☐	☐	☐

	Never	Occasionally	Often
Stares into space	☐	☐	☐
Appetite loss	☐	☐	☐
Sadness	☐	☐	☐
Irritability	☐	☐	☐
Excessive demands for teacher's attention	☐	☐	☐
Destructive	☐	☐	☐
Mood changes quickly and drastically	☐	☐	☐
TOTALS	☐	☐	☐

The sheets above and following could be usefully circulated to parents, GP and Child and Adolescent Mental Health Services (CAMHS)/diagnosing/prescribing clinician. Remember that your feedback could make a difference to the effectiveness of the medication. Because most medication for AD/HD is short-acting, the timing of the dose is important. It needs to be used in conjunction with the demands put on the child for best effect.

Time/Medication Monitoring Form

Name: _____

Week commencing: _____

Monday   Times of tablets _____am _____pm

Level of behavioural concern: 1 low 5 high
10am   1   2   3   4   5
12 noon   1   2   3   4   5
2pm   1   2   3   4   5

Comments on behaviour and emotional state

Tuesday   Times of tablets _____am _____pm

Level of behavioural concern: 1 low 5 high
10am   1   2   3   4   5
12 noon   1   2   3   4   5
2pm   1   2   3   4   5

Comments on behaviour and emotional state

Wednesday   Times of tablets _____am _____pm

Level of behavioural concern: 1 low 5 high
10am   1   2   3   4   5
12 noon   1   2   3   4   5
2pm   1   2   3   4   5

Comments on behaviour and emotional state

Thursday Times of tablets _____am _____pm

Level of behavioural concern: 1 low 5 high

10am	1	2	3	4	5
12 noon	1	2	3	4	5
2pm	1	2	3	4	5

Comments on behaviour and emotional state

Friday Times of tablets _____am _____pm

Level of behavioural concern: 1 low 5 high

10am	1	2	3	4	5
12 noon	1	2	3	4	5
2pm	1	2	3	4	5

Comments on behaviour and emotional state

Form completed

by _____ Date_____

Multimodal support packages

Medication for AD/HD should be used as part of a multimodal support package. Some Child and Adolescent Mental Health Services (CAMHS) will offer counselling, family therapy, cognitive behaviour therapy, psychotherapy, and occupational therapy including sensory integration. There are other therapies which people claim to have been successful in helping to minimize the negative side of AD/HD, for example, the Feingold diet, art therapy, homeopathy, cranial osteopathy, time-line therapy and neuro-linguistic programming. Much improvement can be made where there is a safe routine in the home and school setting, where the child knows the boundaries and where the adults are not so exhausted that they cannot cope with the constant demands made by the child. Support for the adults around the child are essential. Coping alone with an AD/HD child is not a recipe for success. It is sometimes possible to get disability living allowance and carers' allowance for a child with AD/HD. In your role as TA you can act as a listening ear to the parent who is under great stress. You can help to make them feel they are not alone in this situation and can use two heads to solve problems which occur, both in school and at home. You can also become more and more informed and help parents who are only experienced with their own child to see things from different angles. In time you can give a glimmer of light at the end of the tunnel because you will have seen a number of children go along this route. You have a very important educational and pastoral role to play, and you could be of more benefit than anyone else in the support network.

How important is the label?

This is a good question to ask yourself, and sometimes also the family of the child you are working with. Being labelled has both advantages and disadvantages. The label itself cannot be applied until a diagnosis, made by a doctor, has been decided upon. Once a child has a label it is difficult to change. A diagnosis is the only way to get medication for AD/HD, but many of the other aspects of support should be able to be accessed without a diagnosis, provided the AD/HD is not too severe. It is also worth pointing out that strategies like dietary monitoring, good routines, plenty of structured activities and lots of positive behaviour specific feedback, coupled with a good understanding of the condition by all adults around the child, can go a long way to reducing the symptoms of AD/HD in a child before a diagnosis is sought.

The table below shows some of the advantages and disadvantages associated with the label of AD/HD. The list is not exhaustive, and you may be able to think of other advantages and disadvantages you have personally come across.

Advantages	Disadvantages
Enables multiprofessional support including medication	Family may feel pressurized into accepting medication
Gives a reason for behaviour	Gives an excuse for behaviour
Gives school a reason to get specialist training of staff	Stigmatization if people don't understand the condition
Teachers are more sympathetic to the child	Preconceived expectations of behaviour which may not be correct
Gives child better life chances by counselling into appropriate careers	
Shorthand for describing a particular aspect of personality	AD/HD eclipses all other aspects of the child's personality
	Picked on by peers – called names like 'mental'
Label can give status in some circles – AD/HD children tend to be intelligent	
Disability living allowance can sometimes be awarded	
Gives parents a reason for the behaviour and makes them feel less to blame for the behaviour	Parents give up and rely too heavily on support services

Advantages	Disadvantages
Child feels special	Child feels different
	Child feels under pressure to take medication
	Label could last for life and be difficult to get rid of if that was desired later in life
Family better understood by society	Family stigmatized by society

Why diagnose?

In theory a family should be able to access all they need for their child with AD/HD-type behaviour, apart from medication, without having a diagnosis, but by describing the behaviours. However, in practice it is probably easier to access services and benefits with the shorthand of the label AD/HD. Careful consideration, though, needs to be given to the effect the diagnosis may have long term on the child – for the reasons outlined in the section on the label above. In your position as TA you may talk to parents who are unsure where to go for further support. Each case needs to be viewed individually, but initially increasing the understanding of the condition by the adults around the child and consequently altering the way the child is handled may go a long way to relieving the negative symptoms of AD/HD.

Review

Quiz

	Yes	No	Maybe
1 AD/HD can appear at any age	☐	☐	☐
2 AD/HD is diagnosed by a clinical psychologist	☐	☐	☐
3 For a diagnosis of AD/HD the behaviour must be regularly visible in two or more settings for at least six months	☐	☐	☐
4 Stimulant medication helps the AD/HD brain to feel 'satisfied' and therefore calm	☐	☐	☐
5 Common side effects to stimulant medication include weight loss and sleeplessness	☐	☐	☐
6 AD/HD is not a medical condition	☐	☐	☐
7 Medication can have a dramatic positive effect	☐	☐	☐
8 The observations of a TA are very important in helping the clinician make a diagnosis	☐	☐	☐
9 Each AD/HD case needs to be treated individually	☐	☐	☐
10 There is still debate over whether or not medication is better than a combination of behavioural treatment and medication	☐	☐	☐
11 Support for the adults around the child is as important as support for the child themself	☐	☐	☐
12 Being labelled AD/HD has both advantages and disadvantages	☐	☐	☐

Management of AD/HD

This chapter looks at:

- Golden rules for encouraging desirable behaviour
- My Success Book and bespoke behaviour programme writing
- Maximization and minimization conditions
- Neuro-linguistic programming and sensory integration
- Relaxation/yoga

Golden rules for encouraging desirable behaviour

Encouraging desirable behaviour is a full-time job requiring much patience, vigilance and understanding.

1 Use positive teaching strategies

Give five times as much behaviour-specific praise as criticism – not easy, but it works after enough time has elapsed for the child to believe you mean it – this could take a few months.

Case study for golden rule 1: The story of Patrick and Mrs Brown

Some years ago I was asked to go to look at Patrick. Patrick was exhibiting quite severely disruptive behaviour in school. He was about eight at the time. For some reason there had been quite a delay in the time between the initial request to see him had been made and the time when the paperwork got to my desk. First I had a meeting with his carer, Maggie, who was a relative on his father's side. She told me all about what he was like at home, how difficult he was, how first his mum had left the family home, and now he never saw his father either. I duly made the appointment with the school to go and do some preliminary observations of him in class, which would then be followed by discussions with his teacher and TAs. Ideas would come from these discussions about how to proceed in class, whether to use a behaviour programme, whether to try changing some practice that the adults were employing. Working as a team, we could have come up with many things. However, in this case things were different.

I went into the classroom to do my observation and found Patrick placed in a seat at the front of the class quite close to where the teacher, Mrs Brown, gravitated. On the wall there was a massive display showing all of the rewards children were gaining for their endeavours, both academic and behavioural. While in the room I became aware of an almost magical presence. I don't remember hearing one negative comment from Mrs Brown. She had the whole class in the palm of her hand, she lead them as opposed to pushing them. She encouraged and valued every child and, as far as Patrick was concerned, there was no evidence of the difficult behaviour I had been told he engaged in. Always when you go in as a visitor to do an observation you have to be aware that your presence in the room will be having some kind of effect on the behaviour there. Sometimes it is positive and sometimes it is negative. I needed to determine if Patrick was one of those children who responded well to having someone new in the room and if this good behaviour was unusual.

My observations then had shown that Patrick was very happy in this class, and was doing well, he was on task the vast majority of the time, in fact more so than the average in the class.

At the end of the lesson I was able to speak with Mrs Brown and ask her whether or not the behaviour I had seen was normal, and she confirmed that it was and that she found him to be a bright member of the class who was responding well.

I walked away from the room almost unable to hold back the tears. The practice I had just seen was exemplary. Mrs Brown was making a massive difference to this boy's life. My acid test is always 'Would I like this teacher to teach my own child?' and the answer here was a big 'Yes, please!!!!'

Mrs Brown's secret wasn't really that top secret, it was just that she employed the principles of positive teaching in a genuine and sincere way. She loved her class and each child in it, for being themselves, and they loved her back and rewarded her with great behaviour and good achievement.

Some time later I saw Patrick again, he was with a different teacher, his behaviour problems had come back, and he had been diagnosed AD/HD and was taking a heavy dose of Ritalin that didn't seem to be helping very much.

2 Act as if you are patient

Eventually you will become the way you behave – try to smile inside.

Case study for golden rule 2: Jenny acts 'as if'

Sometimes when we need to do something we are not too sure about, we waver and don't actually do that thing. Other times we find it hard to do something because inside we are boiling up and we just don't want to do it. What we project to other people, we tend to get back. So if we want calm, patient children we need to project calm, patient behaviour.

Jenny was a teacher in a middle school. She had a lot of children with behaviour difficulties to teach and sometimes she had her patience tried to the utmost degree. But Jenny knew a little bit about neuro-linguistic programming from a one-day introduction for teachers she had been on. She had been taught that when you need to do something that you really don't want to do you can visualize someone doing that thing really really well and model what they do. Jenny visualized the face of Barbara in *The Good Life* when she was having to be very patient with Tom's latest silly idea. She pictured that serene look and the lovely smile, and she modelled this in her class with her difficult children when they were doing their best to try her patience. The results were miraculous. Not only did it calm the pupils down, but Jenny also felt calm and really did become more patient with her class. It was as if this moment of patience gave the emotional temperature in the classroom time to fall and everyone benefited from a second or two of the calm it seemed to introduce.

3 Avoid getting drawn into confrontation

At times it is very difficult to avoid getting involved in a discussion that quickly turns into argument and bickering. It is useful here to be able to take a step back and look at your own emotional state – steer clear of getting drawn into an 'adolescent exchange'.

Activity

Think about your own childhood, your experience as a parent or carer, your experience as a TA, and any other experience you may have had with young people. Try to think of times when you got involved in arguments or bickering. How did they resolve? What did you learn from these experiences?

Hopefully you will have reflected on those times and will now be better able to work out which battles are worth fighting and which just are not worth taking the risk on. Pettiness and point scoring doesn't set good examples for young people to follow. Put yourself in the position of the young person. You may be able to see how it is largely up to the adult to ensure these squabbles do not escalate. Never forget that despite how threatening some young people appear to be they are in an inferior position in society and will themselves be unconsciously threatened by an adult who is hostile towards them. This will elicit a basic fight or flight response. Each one of us at all times has to be aware of how basic instincts and unconscious processes affect how we act and how others act towards us.

4 Seek opportunities for discussing cases with other colleagues in a problem-solving way – always respecting the child

Case study for golden rule 4: Adequate supervision for adults around the child

Before I came into the education profession I worked for a major child care charity, although not a social worker myself (I was actually a fund raiser) I spent a lot of time at projects with social workers learning more about the work I was going out raising money for. I was very impressed by one project I spent a few days with. Every Friday they saw no clients but spent part of the day in 'supervision'. The clients were families with some big problems, domestic violence and sexual abuse were commonplace. On Friday afternoon the project workers were expected to bring cases to the team for a group supervision session. A worker would describe a case, the rest of the team would listen and ask questions to clarify the facts, then the worker who had brought the case would sit out of the circle and listen to the discussion the team had about what they had just heard. The discussion was able to go in a direction it would not have been able to had the presenter still been able to talk – they would have kept dragging the discussion back in line with their own patterning. After about

10 or 15 minutes of discussion the presenter would be brought back into the circle and given the opportunity to comment on what had been said. Frequently the comment is made that new ideas have come up from the 'group mind' and new ways forward with difficult problems are found.

In education we have no proper structure for the kind of 'supervision' that the other helping professions know is so important. Social workers who find themselves working in education are amazed by this. They wonder how can teachers and TAs who have to deal with the multitude of emotional fallout day in day out manage to do their jobs effectively. And the truth is, if they don't have the right kind of support, they won't be able to. It might look OK from the outside, but think about the internal stress levels of the teacher, and think about what the children in their classes are having to put up with.

5 Be consistent

Be consistent in all you do with the child. Again, this is a difficult task, and you will need support to be able to do this. Consistency is most effective when all adults around the child act as a well-practised team, playing to the same rules and behaving in a predictable, loving and fair way. This way the child begins to be able to trust the adults around him and can develop the strength to work on his own behaviour control.

6 Set up behaviour programmes in consultation with the child

My Success Book consists of a book and an individually tailored programme to suit each child. The principle behind the programme is that the child negotiates their own goals and their own rewards. My Success Book is the first part of the process where a number of discussions take place between yourself and the child about their behaviour and who their behaviour most affects, then the behaviour most easy to alter is chosen by the child as the first goal of the behaviour programme. The next stage in the process is for the child to select a picture they would like on their success plan sheet. This can be anything traceable, or if you or they are good at art anything they like that you or they can draw. The picture they have chosen is then split into segments of the day. The size of the segment depends on the child, but will normally be no more than 15 minutes. This sounds labour intensive, as at the end of every 15-minute period a behaviour check has to be made and signed for, but it's worth it. This is then followed by the child choosing some rewards. Rewards are given for cumulative not consecutive effort, so avoiding the sudden-death effect of some behaviour programmes. With this programme it is always worth having another go at behaving well.

My Success Book is explained in more detail later in this chapter.

7 Provide a secure environment

An emotionally and physically secure environment with clear behavioural boundaries provides an environment that gives freedom within a framework of discipline – this will ensure the child feels safe because the boundaries are clearly set, but free to express themselves and learn. Use the needs audit derived from Maslow's hierarchy of needs to help ensure the basic needs are met.

8 Develop excellent listening skills

Listening is something that is hard to do in school. The pace of school life is so fast that frequently adults find it very hard to practise good listening. Keep this in mind, and the next time you are tempted to mind-read what a child means and finish off their sentence for them try to refrain! It's true not everyone does this, but it's a good idea to be aware that it does happen, and a lot of children feel they are just heard. The Chinese symbol for 'to listen' (following page) encapsulates very well how we need to use our eyes, ears and heart to give undivided attention.

ears

eyes

heart

to give undivided attention

9 Build a relationship and hold the child in mind

Take a personal interest in the child's interests and show the child that you think about them when they are not about. Relationships are crucial to happiness and a good learning environment.

10 Keep your sense of humour

This will help you to keep open the channels of communication which once broken are hard to repair – and it might keep your stress level down as well. Sometimes you don't win every game, but if it was a fair match, played by the rules, you might go away feeling some sense of satisfaction and a desire to play again. Have you ever noticed how, if you can laugh about something, any problem you had just does not seem so bad? Keeping your sense of humour where AD/HD children are concerned can sometimes be very easy, because they are often very very funny. However, sometimes when they are being rude and defiant towards you, it can get a little difficult to see the funny side of things. However hard it might seem, don't take their negative comments personally and always keep your sense of humour. Remember Jenny who acted as if she was patient. Try acting as if you have a sense of humour even when you have lost it.

My Success Book

 My name

 My address

 My school

 My teacher

I live with these people:

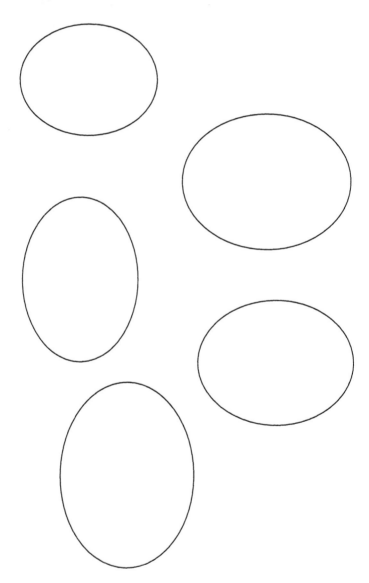

I am good at these things:

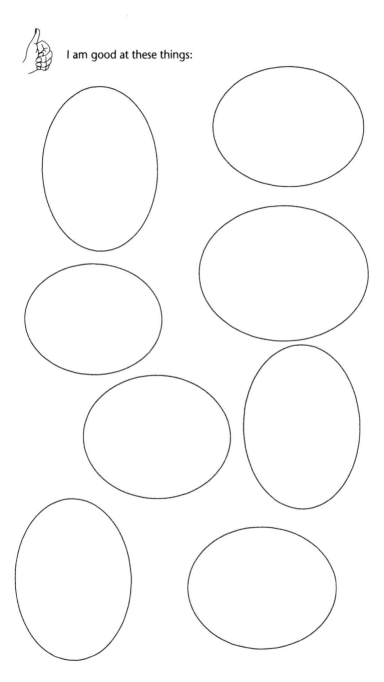

Sometimes I do things that other people don't like me to do, like:

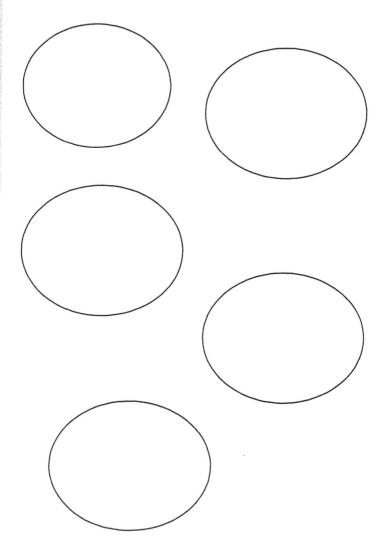

The Teaching Assistant's Guide to AD/HD

The people who get upset by these things are:

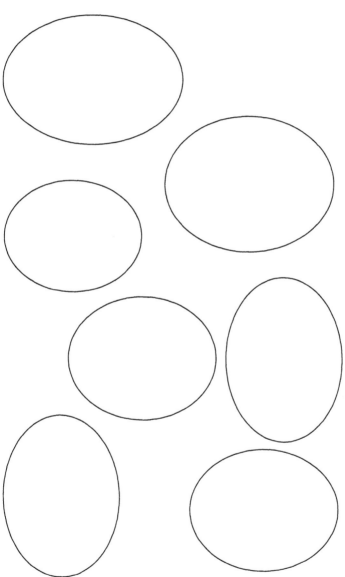

The person who is most upset by what I do is:

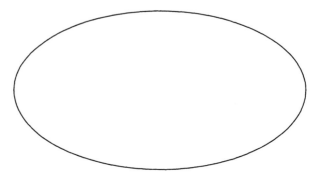

 Three things I do that upset other people that I would like to change are:

1 _____

_____

_____

2 _____

_____

_____

3 _____

_____

_____

The ones I think would be easiest to change are:

The rewards I would like for changing are

My Certificate of Success

Thumbs up to

_____

_____

who has changed his/her behaviour

Signed

_____

Class teacher

Signed

_____

Teaching Assistant

Signed

_____

Headteacher

Date

_____

You will see from My Success Book that the objective is to enable the child to talk a little about themselves, where they live, who they live with, what they are good at, before they move on to thinking about the behaviours they exhibit that other people are not too keen on. They then are guided to think about the people these behaviours might be affecting, and most of all to think about the person who is most affected by the behaviour, i.e. themselves, because they are the only person who is always with that behaviour. We are aiming for a 'buy in' here and a feeling that they own the programme, not you, so the language used here needs to be very non-judgemental and the task of drawing out may take a lot of patience. The child needs to come to conclusions without you saying the words for them. It may take a few sessions to get to where you need to be before you start the programme. My Success Book is as much about the non-judgemental relationship between you and the child as it is about the child making the effort to change. It is important for the same person to follow the process through with the child. The next task is to think about which of the behaviours would be the easiest to change, and use that as the target. At this point it is imperative to ensure success, so the target needs to be achievable for the majority of the day. The next stage is to look together for a picture that the child likes. Trace the picture and split the day into 15-minute segments. This normally pans out at 25 in a day. Include breaks and lunchtime. As each 15-minute period goes by a behaviour check is made and if the child is complying with the target you initial the segment. If for example the requirement is to stay in seat, then so long as they are in their seat at times when it is required they get the credit. If it is break or lunch they get the credits free as there is no requirement to stay in your seat at that time so not to award the credit would penalize them unfairly. This way the child should pick up quite a few credits and start to feel that they actually do have some control over their behaviour. If the child believes they can do it there is a much greater chance that they will be able to do it, so our job is to give them that confidence. Each day the child should be scoring between 15 and 20 credits. If not the target is

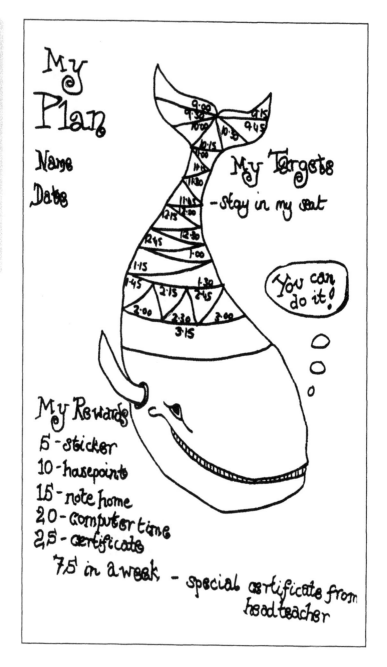

too hard to achieve and needs to be changed slightly. You will see from the picture of the behaviour programme – My Plan (below) – Whale version – that an extra reward for good effort throughout the week is put in to help with training for longer-term incentives – an area of great difficulty for the AD/HD child. In the plan below the reward is a certificate from the head teacher, but this would be negotiated with the child – it may be that some free time was more valued. Also, the rewards are given as soon as 5, 10, 15, etc., and segments are signed cumulatively *not* consecutively. Remember whatever else the child has done that day, if they have complied with the target they get the reward. This programme focuses on one small target, one small step at a time, and is not dependent on good behaviour across the board. It is dependent on building in success for the child and helping them to recognize and savour what it feels like to get things right. The programme is deliberately hand-drawn in conference with the child as it is the child's very own programme that no one else has had before.

Any behaviour programme will only work for a short period of time before it needs refreshing. Another way which sometimes works with AD/HD children, but at first might seem rather negative, is the response-cost version. Here the child has a bank of tokens at the beginning of the day (for older children, the week may be appropriate), which are forfeited for unwanted behaviour. This works well with children who find it difficult to work towards a goal, and who have stronger sense of preserving what they already have than gaining something they do not yet have. Always try the positive method first.

Whenever you stop using a particular reward system make sure you keep up the behaviour-specific praise.

Maximization and minimization conditions

There is no doubt that the negative behaviours associated with AD/HD can be either minimized of maximized according to the environment within which the child finds themself. Any parent of an AD/HD child will agree that plenty of space will help.

AD/HD children tend to be noisy and this has a knock-on effect on neighbour relations. Families who are living in cramped conditions close to other families are very likely to suffer complaints about their AD/HD child's behaviour. Jackie Fletcher (1999) in her diary of an AD/HD parent reveals how both neighbours put their houses up for sale, because – she suspected – of the disturbances her son was causing. Another family moved into a house in a rural area surrounded by fields in an attempt to give their child space to grow and express himself without attracting too much unwanted attention from neighbours. Of course this is an option open to only the lucky few due to funding restrictions. Lack of funds will also impact on the range of activities the child can engage in. However, a child with a diagnosis of AD/HD, is likely to be able to attract disability living allowance, some of which could be used to pay for activities such as swimming, karate, badminton, trampolining, football, etc., which are all useful for channelling the energy and for socialization. It is, however, likely that an AD/HD child will quickly tire of any activity. Perseverance is essential here. Start children early on these activities and they are likely to be able to get used to the rules required to stay in the group before they look like downright disruptive adolescents.

Another device that has been seen to be of use in helping the AD/HD child to grow through the difficult years is that of keeping pets. Dogs, geese, rabbits have all proved to be loyal companions, sometimes helping to compensate for the friendships that are so difficult to keep with the peer group. A lively dog can not only be a friend and companion, but also a good way of keeping fit.

Single parents endeavouring to rear a family without support from other understanding adults leads to frayed tempers, and parenting by crisis management becomes the order of the day. Rather than the parent being in a position of providing emotional security for the family, the parent becomes the one who is crying out for nurture because of the immensity of the task of bringing up a family affected by AD/HD.

With any child the parent needs to be at least one step ahead, with AD/HD you need to be many, many steps ahead as they move so fast. Constant vigilance and intelligent strategic planning is needed to ensure situations do not arise that will cause friction and chaos. It is very hard, demanding and exhausting. Getting on top of the situation must be done early. Early diagnosis/identification is of great benefit here.

Probably one of the biggest barriers to minimizing the negative side of AD/HD is the attitude exhibited towards the family by society in general.

Jane's story

Jane's son Harry, whom we met earlier, poses Jane with day by day, minute by minute difficulties. She has an exhausting regime including swimming, karate, tennis. She takes him to the local country park where the rangers do sessions with young people as often as there are available sessions; she usually takes a few other children too. She encourages him to play with friends, but ensures that the friends are not in his company for too long at a time. Jane has always tried to ensure Harry has a balanced diet, he is not allowed cola unless it's a high day or holiday, and he eats good food, for example, pasta with sauces including food-processed vegetables to ensure he eats the vegetables but doesn't necessarily know he is – less arguments that way. Jane recalls how she used to have to massage Harry's head when they had to wait in a queue anywhere, this seemed to soothe him and just give her a minute or two of extra calm. Many times Jane had felt the pressure of other adults when she was out and about. Shopping at the supermarket was something she avoided doing with Harry unless there was absolutely no alternative. He would scream and writhe about in the trolley when he was younger, and when too big for that it was impossible for her to stop him from running around the store. She felt the pressure from people as they looked at her with daggers in their eyes and she felt she could hear them saying 'Get control over your child, you bad parent.'

Before Jane had Harry she had ideas about parenting. First there would be no dummy, secondly he would be breast-fed up to six months, third, good routines would be quickly established (like the bedtime routine), fourth, she would involve him in as wide a range of activities as possible and continue to socialize, fifth, he would never eat junk food. These were just a few of her ideas. Within hours of a difficult birth, a howling, unhappy baby was soothed by a dummy, which was to stay with him until he was established at school, and even later at night. Breast feeding only continued for 10 weeks. He was seemingly impossible to routinize, with sleep being a very evasive state for him, and once asleep any tiny creak of a floorboard or breath seemed to wake him up again. Visiting friends became an impossibility because nothing was safe and eating out was accompanied by Jane being molested by Harry who persisted in crawling all over her as she tried to eat. One way to buy a little tiny window in which to eat out was to go to a place where they sell lots of lovely junk food and have a ball park for the children to play in while the parents flop in exhaustion for 60 seconds.

So Jane's ideas about parenting were swiftly kicked into touch by the real experience of living with AD/HD. Luckily she had some good support and advice around her, and was given respite. She also had enough money to be able to take Harry to various activities. Swimming proved to be a problem at first because the teacher reported he just didn't seem to be listening and recommended he leave the class. Undaunted, Jane continued to take him herself, and later found another class that had fewer children in, was more expensive, but seemed to be better able to cope with Harry, and he did learn to swim quite well. Jane and her extended family put an immense amount of energy into the early years with Harry, and to read comments in the paper that there is no such thing as AD/HD, or to be faced with school and NHS staff who just describe your child as naughty and give you that 'it's all down to poor parenting look' really does not help.

> [Jane said] Sometimes the pressure from other people when you are out trying to wait in a queue for something and your child is climbing the walls, with another parent looking at you as though you are dirt and a bad parent, sometimes pushes you into a negative exchange with your child, not because you think that is the right thing to do for them, but because you feel under pressure from the onlookers. A wedge then gets driven between you and your child. That wedge could stay far longer than the onlooker is going to be bothered about what you and your child are doing.

Ways Jane found to maximize on good behaviour
Giving instructions
Jane learned that there are some ways to make things easier. First she appreciated that it was often hard for Harry to follow instructions. She knew it wasn't an understanding problem as such – he was a very bright boy – but she observed that if she ensured she was standing in front of him and close to him when she gave him an instruction she was far more likely to get compliance, also she would sometimes get him to repeat the instruction back to her, but not if they were in a situation where this would cause embarrassment. She also realized that one instruction at a time was better than a lot. Give one instruction, let him carry it out, then move on to the next. She always tried to look patient on the outside, even when she was tearing her hair out on the inside. She had also noticed that although she was able to get direct eye contact most of the time from Harry, other people found this difficult and sometimes took it as a sign of a lack of respect. In fact it was Harry's shyness and poor self-esteem that was preventing him looking people in the eye. Harry went to two different schools

where he was consistently in trouble for his behaviour. At his third primary school Jane was able to discuss with the school how she worked with Harry, and most of his teachers worked well with her to enable him to thrive in that school.

Ways to reward good behaviour
One of the things his new teacher was very good at was giving positive behaviour-specific feedback – in other words praise that actually tells the child what it is they have done that is good. This way he had a good chance of being able to repeat the good behaviour. She also sat him close to her in the classroom so he felt secure there. She took a big interest in him as a person, not just a member of the class. She would talk to him about the things he had done at the weekend – she was 'holding him in mind'. It is so important for children to feel that we are thinking about them even when they are not with us. Jane observed that Harry was getting lots of praise for his good behaviour and although he was still doing some pretty daft things in school most of that behaviour was ignored by his teacher at the time, but he was given gentle timely and subtle reminders about how to act in particular situations so that the behaviour was avoided next time. This way his self-esteem was preserved, and he was able to develop some good behaviour patterns which were to help him in the future.

Summary of ways to maximize desirable behaviour

Giving instructions
- ensure you have gained the child's attention – stand in front if necessary
- do not insist the child makes direct eye contact – this may be too difficult and counterproductive
- because of short-term memory difficulties give brief and clear instructions – one stage at a time – wait for it to be done – then give the next

- repeat the instruction in a calm and friendly way
- give the child a discrete cue to begin work
- try providing one instruction at a time in large print
- explain the purpose of the work and how it is meant to look when finished
- suggest an appropriate amount of time to be spent on each task

Ways of rewarding good behaviour

- use verbal praise – you always have this with you
- make it behaviour-specific if you can – then the child knows what they have done well and can do it again in future. Subsequently give reminders of the successful action
- use a 'response-cost' system where the child has a bank of tokens at the beginning of the week/day which are forfeited for unwanted behaviour. This works well with children who find difficulty working towards a reward a long way off
- use very small time slots to monitor behaviour – 5, 10 or 15 minutes
- give rewards for cumulative good behaviour
- change the reward frequently as interest will wane
- change the system if the child has to wait too long for a reward, or is getting too many
- keep up praise even when tangible reward systems have ceased

Discouraging undesirable behaviour – pretending to ignore

- pretend to ignore undesirable behaviour if it is not too dangerous or disruptive – avoid making eye contact, look calm, and don't laugh however funny it seems, busy yourself with something and don't get drawn into discussion about the behaviour
- when the behaviour has ceased resume normal relations

Discouraging undesirable behaviour – time out

- when behaviour is too dangerous or disruptive to ignore, use 'time out'
- the aim of 'time out' is to remove the child from where he is receiving reinforcement for the inappropriate behaviour – *not* to create discomfort or fear in the child
- the child should stay in 'time out' until calm
- do not demand an apology at the end of 'time out'. Be friendly and matter of fact
- always ensure that the child gets sufficient 'quality time' with you and does not have to resort to acting out to get your attention
- promoting positive interactions is essential
- be as consistent as you possibly can be in your interactions with the child
- look at changing the environment before you try to change the child – it is usually much easier and can be very effective

In the playground

- supervise adequately to pre-empt problems but make supervision subtle
- talk to the child about getting on with others
- provide opportunities for individualized non-competitive activities

Neuro-linguistic programming, sensory integration and AD/HD

What is neuro-linguistic programming (NLP)

Imagine being able to understand unconscious communication, and how to communicate with the unconscious. Listening to the language people use gives you clues as to how they process language. If you can mirror their style more accurately, you can enhance your communication with them, so you can harmonize with them, and draw out the learning more effectively.

The founders of NLP, John Grinder and Richard Bandler, studied the communication styles of very gifted communicators and modelled their behaviour. They found amazing and interesting results. By modelling the way excellent communicators work, anyone can improve their communication skills, and for human beings communication is like lifeblood. Who wouldn't want to improve their communication skills?

The basis of success in school is a good relationship with the child. An invaluable starting point for building a good relationship quickly is to attain good rapport with the other person. Basic NLP introduces ways of doing this effortlessly and unconsciously. By learning about the way people take information in, which senses seem to be dominant, and how they communicate by observing their preferred communication style, you can build up good rapport and a good relationship quickly.

Did you know that it is estimated we have over 2 million bits of information coming to us every second. The human brain is capable of taking in far less than this at any one time so a lot has to be ignored. It actually chunks information into 7 plus or minus 2 chunks. More than that and it feels like overload.

A piece of information comes to us in a variety of forms, it could be visual (sight), auditory (sound), kinaesthetic (touch), olfactory (smell), gustatory (taste) or even something we say to ourselves – auditory digital.

We have a number of filters that take the experience and translate it into an internal representation – in a way we are talking to ourselves at this point. This is how we as individuals make sense of the basic information the senses give us. Our interpretations will differ from those of the next person not because they are right and we are wrong or vice versa, but because we are all different, have different filters, different experiences, different memories, beliefs and attitudes. In NLP there is a saying 'The map is not the territory', meaning the internal representations that we make about an event are not necessarily what actually happened.

To cope, our brain looks for recognizable patterns in

information, then deletes, distorts and generalizes the information. What we perceive is what we create. We project out what we have left in our filter systems, after filtering.

Sensory integration (SI)

In some ways NLP goes hand in hand with sensory integration because of the focus on multisensory communication. Sensory integration is a theory pioneered by Dr Jean Ayres in the 1950s. She felt that difficulties faced by neurologically disabled children and adults could be better explained in terms of how the brain processes sensation. Jean Ayres (1979) found that by directing and controlling the input of different senses children can learn and organize behaviour more effectively – this has clear implications for AD/HD as organization is a key skill often evading the AD/HD child. Sensory integration recognizes not five, but seven senses – the extra ones being proprioception – where you are in space – and vestibular – balance. A child with sensory integration problems may appear to find work in school hard to accomplish, to be clumsy, be slow at changing for PE, have difficulty remembering instructions, be hypersensitive to certain situations, be hyperactive and distractable. Clearly again we are seeing links with AD/HD.

So what has all this got to do with AD/HD? AD/HD children, due to their defects in neurotransmission systems, often perceive and react to things in a way slightly different from the norm. To be useful to an AD/HD child you need to be able to get under their skin, i.e. achieve reliable empathy. NLP and SI can be used to work out the child's communication style, build good rapport with them and be able to communicate excellently with them. If you can know what sensory stimulus calms them and what alerts them, what will put them into a learning mood, and what will not, you have a much greater chance of success. Also you will be more able to cope with the difficult behaviour and not take it as a personal affront, but as a method of communication, possibly at that time the only one the child sees as available to them.

Activity: Looking at your own alerting and calming techniques

Imagine you are in a lecture that bores you. What kind of things do you do to keep yourself awake and interested?

_____

_____

_____

_____

_____

_____

_____

Imagine it is Friday teatime and you are anxious about something to do with work about which you can do nothing until Monday morning. What kinds of things do you do to calm yourself down?

_____

_____

_____

_____

_____

_____

_____

You will notice you have a list of completely different things on each side of your paper. If you were able to swap papers with a colleague you would find you not only had different things on each side of the paper, but that your list differed from your colleagues. Imagine looking at the lists made by the whole class, all would have something slightly different on them. So, you see, it is very important to observe each child and work out what it is that that individual needs to feel in a comfortable state to learn. You can use the kind of information gained from the simple exercise above to help you create good learning environments. It is important to realize that we all have different ways of coping with ourselves, and in the classroom we see children trying to find ways to cope with how they feel. Sometimes their methods aren't too useful for everyone else, but our job is to help them find ways of coping that meet their needs as well as not impacting too negatively on everyone else. This requires negotiation.

Both NLP and SI are massive topics to which justice cannot be done here. If you think they are something you would like to learn more about further information is available by emailing katespohrer@hotmail.com.

Guided relaxation

Relaxation can be effectively used with AD/HD children, but time needs to be invested in getting them trained. Do not expect to be able to carry out a full relaxation quickly. Start with a simple standing exercise from yoga called tadasana. Tell the child you are going to teach them how to stand, that usually gets them interested because they think they know all about that already, what could you possibly teach them? Once they have got the hang of it you can look for and praise good standing. Use the Sanskrit term tadasana. They will soon catch on to this special way of standing and be able to reproduce it in other situations under your guidance. Initially you will only be able to get compliance for a very short period of time, possibly only seconds, but keep persevering and gradually extend the time, but never set up to fail.

Tadasana

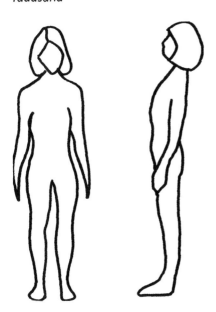

Stand up straight and still. Feet should be directly below the hips so feet are hip width apart. Heels and toes should be parallel. Feel your feet taking the weight of your body. Be aware of how wide they are. Allow the feet to be soft. Shake out tension from your arms and hands and let them drop by your sides. Look straight ahead, balance the head on the top neckbones, tuck the chin in, relax. Imagine a piece of string attached to the top of your head gently pulling up to the sky, as you do this you will grow a little and your backbone will stretch a little. Keeping your neck, jaw and shoulders relaxed, maintain the pose for a few breaths. No one should hear you breathe. In . . . out . . . in . . . out . . .

Encourage children to practise tadasana every time they are waiting in a line, you will be surprised at the difference standing like this can make.

Healing sunlight

You can do this exercise either in tadasana or sitting on a chair. If sitting,

- ensure that both feet flat are on the floor
- make sure that the back is straight and bottom is as far back into the seat as it will comfortably go
- rest hands, palms facing upwards, on the thighs

Begin thinking about your breathing.

Close your eyes.

Breathe in quietly – no one should be able to hear you breathe.

Breathe out quietly.

In . . .

Out . . .

In . . .

Out . . .

Imagine your body to be full of dark blue ink. That ink is all the negative things that have happened to you recently, all the arguments and cross words you have had, all the nasty things people have said to you . . . or you have said to them.

On every in-breath imagine that the blue ink is being pushed down your body and is being changed into golden sunlight.

In . . . your head now fills with bright sunlight . . . out

In . . . your shoulders fill with bright sunlight . . . out

In . . . your arms fill with bright sunlight . . . out

In . . . your chest fills with bright sunlight . . . out

In . . . your tummy fills with bright sunlight . . . out

In . . . your thighs fill with bright sunlight . . . out

In . . . your knees and calves fill with bright sunlight . . . out

In . . . your ankles and feet fill with bright sunlight . . . out

Now you have drained all of the blue ink of bad feelings down to your toes and out into a big puddle next to you on the ground . . .

Close by there is a drain, the ink trickles toward the drain and disappears down the drain . . . away . . . leaving you feeling glowing and good . . .

Enjoy that feeling for a few more breaths.

Slowly remember where you are . . . (in school, classroom . . .)

Keeping your eyes closed, rub your hands together, place your warm hands over your eyes, open your eyes behind your hands, slowly spread out your fingers to let in the light.

How did that feel?

Review

Quiz

		Yes	No	Maybe
1	Taking a step back helps to lower the emotional temperature in a potentially confrontational situation	☐	☐	☐
2	Consistent handling of AD/HD children is key to success	☐	☐	☐
3	Behaviour programmes need to be negotiated with and individually tailored to suit the child	☐	☐	☐
4	Small, quick rewards for being on task for short periods of time will work better than long-term goals	☐	☐	☐
5	When giving AD/HD children instructions it is best to give them in small chunks and get the child to repeat them	☐	☐	☐
6	Building a non-judgemental relationship with an AD/HD child is essential to helping them understand themselves and improve their behaviour	☐	☐	☐
7	Always insist on direct eye contact when talking to a child with AD/HD	☐	☐	☐
8	If you act as if you are patient, in time you may become more patient	☐	☐	☐
9	The environment an AD/HD child finds themselves in has no impact on their behaviour	☐	☐	☐

	Yes	No	Maybe

10 Relaxation and yoga techniques have never been found to be of use to AD/HD children

☐ ☐ ☐

11 Giving five times as much behaviour-specific praise as criticism is hard but well worth it

☐ ☐ ☐

12 Using very small time slots of 5, 10, 15 minutes to monitor behaviour is unlikely to help an AD/HD child improve their behaviour

☐ ☐ ☐

13 A good sense of humour that enables you to laugh at yourself, and with others, not at them, helps a lot in behaviour management

☐ ☐ ☐

14 Undesirable behaviour should never be ignored but always corrected

☐ ☐ ☐

15 'Time out' is used to create discomfort and fear in a child

☐ ☐ ☐

16 Always try to change the child's behaviour before trying to change the environment

☐ ☐ ☐

17 Neuro-linguistic programming uses rapport building and sensory acuity to enable better behaviour management

☐ ☐ ☐

18 Sensory Integration is a theory of directing and controlling the input of different senses

☐ ☐ ☐

	Yes	No	Maybe

19 To help prepare a child for work find out what activities help to calm and what help to alert them to get them into a receptive learning state ☐ ☐ ☐

20 Using the 'group mind' can help sort out new ways of working with young people with AD/HD ☐ ☐ ☐

Review

Think back to the beginning of this book when you were introduced to the group of AD/HD children. Go back and have a look at them, right now, if you like. Think too about what you have read, and choose one of the case studies to apply what you have learned in this book. You will be bringing in all sorts of learnings from way, way before you picked up this book, but throughout the process of reading, your unconscious mind will have been piecing things together for you and enabling you to employ new methods, think new thoughts and break through limiting beliefs you might have had in the past about what you could and couldn't do with children. Your mind is very creative and you have the ability to solve many problems if you just allow yourself to do so.

Questions to ask yourself

About the child

1   Have you discussed how it feels for them in the classroom?

_____

2   Is there a behaviour-monitoring programme in place?

_____

3 If there is a behaviour-monitoring programme, have the targets and rewards been derived jointly by yourself and the pupil?

_____

4 Have accurate observations of concentration span been carried out so that short enough time spans for the behaviour programme can be set?

_____

5 Have you observed and discussed which tasks are of interest to the child?

_____

6 Have you observed what helps the child to get into a receptive state for working?

_____

7 Is the child's level of concentration affected by the time and events of the day?

_____

8 How is such an effect taken into account when planning tasks for the child?

_____

9 If medication is used are dose times taken into account when planning tasks for the child?

_____

10 What kinds of tasks does the child work best on? Can more of these be built into the curriculum?

_____

11 Does the child need to doodle or fiddle with an object while listening to the speaker?

12 Have hearing, sight and language checks been carried out recently to rule out problems in these areas?

13 What is your relationship with the child like? How do you show that you are holding the child in mind when you are away from them?

14 Do you run a 'Circle of Friends'-type programme (Maines and Robinson 1998) to help this child make and maintain friendships?

15 Is there a skill the child has that can be used to help the school community, thus developing responsibility and self-esteem?

16 Do you maintain your sense of humour at all times?

About classroom organization/teaching styles

1 Have you audited which situations create less concentration and attention problems and which create more? How could you/do you do this?

2 Does the child work at a clear desk?

3 Do you use good role models and peer mentors to work with the child in lessons?

_____

4 Do you ensure that the child is sitting away from distractions like windows, switches, etc?

_____

5 Is the child sure about what is allowed and what isn't, i.e. when it is appropriate to get out of seat and when not?

_____

6 Are these parameters consistently enforced in the classroom?

_____

7 Is the child allowed to work in a quiet place away from others?

_____

8 Have you thought about using a sand timer to help the child time tasks?

_____

9 Is the child able to be assessed using a variety of methods other than written?

_____

10 Is the child able to sit in a place that enables the best chance of success?

_____

11 Do you ensure that the child can see the white board easily (without turning round)?

_____

I hope you have had a go at the quizzes at the end of each chapter. Below are some points for discussion arising from the quizzes. You may feel you have differing views on some of them. If you have any further questions about AD/HD I would be very pleased to hear from you at katespohrer@hotmail.com.

Chapter 1 Review – Quiz answers

	Yes	No	Maybe
1 A condition like AD/HD was described by medics over 100 years ago. *Dr G. F. Still in* The Lancet *described a similar condition*	✓	☐	☐
2 Almost everyone shows AD/HD type behaviour at times. *Particularly at times of stress/anxiety*	✓	☐	☐
3 Some studies estimate the occurrence of AD/HD is around 25 per cent. *Studies indicate a 5 per cent rate*	☐	✓	☐
4 AD/HD is not a medical condition and can be diagnosed by an educational or clinical psychologist. *It is defined as a medical condition and can only be diagnosed by a clinician. However it can be identified by any of us*	☐	✓	☐
5 Not all AD/HD children are hyper-active. *Some are hypoactive, but will still have concentration problems*	✓	☐	☐

	Yes	No	Maybe

6 AD/HD is less diagnosed in girls than in boys because the diagnostic criteria are biased towards boyish behaviour patterns.
There is pressure for a different set of criteria for girls as their AD/HD behaviour tends to show itself in a different way

Yes ✓

7 For AD/HD to be diagnosed the problem behaviours must have been seen before the age of 5.
Diagnostic criteria state before the age of 7, not 5

No ✓

8 Sexual promiscuity in teenage girls can be a sign of AD/HD.
This can be a characteristic

Maybe ✓

9 One of the biggest problems for an AD/HD child is lack of understanding of how the AD/HD brain works and a negative attitude shown by society

Yes ✓

10 AD/HD children find concentrating difficult at times

Yes ✓

11 One of the most infuriating characteristics of AD/HD is that one minute you can be having an adult-level conversation and the next the child can be bouncing round the classroom like a powerball

Yes ✓

	Yes	No	Maybe

12 Children with AD/HD are usually excellent timekeepers and start their work quickly.
Timekeeping is an executive function – an area where there are usually problems for AD/HD people

    [ ] Yes [✓] No [ ] Maybe

13 Because of social clumsiness children with AD/HD can find it hard to keep friends.
They can often be too talkative, boisterous, bossy or tactless to keep friends

    [✓] Yes [ ] No [ ] Maybe

14 AD/HD has an evolutionary function.
We need people in society who are fearless and will push boundaries, but some aspects of this trait are less useful at certain times in man's evolutionary development

    [✓] Yes [ ] No [ ] Maybe

15 Children with AD/HD are often hypercritical of themselves and have low self-esteem

    [✓] Yes [ ] No [ ] Maybe

16 Children with AD/HD are usually of below average intelligence.
They are usually above average and frequently creative and gifted

    [ ] Yes [✓] No [ ] Maybe

17 Some children with AD/HD seem as though they cannot stop talking

    [✓] Yes [ ] No [ ] Maybe

	Yes	No	Maybe

18 Some children with AD/HD choose to sit quietly at the back of the room and keep out of social interactions ☑ ☐ ☐

19 Children with AD/HD will often engage in boundary-testing behaviour ☑ ☐ ☐

20 For AD/HD to be diagnosed the problem behaviours must have been regularly seen in at least two settings, i.e. home and school ☑ ☐ ☐

Chapter 2 Review – Quiz answers

1 Some medications and foods trigger AD/HD type behaviour. ☑ ☐ ☐
Among others, medications for epilepsy have been known to cause AD/HD-type behaviour. Drinks such as cola are well known for their stimulative effects, and some children can have adverse reactions to dairy and wheat products and salicilates – including tomatoes. Foods considered to be good for you like oranges have also been reported to cause problems, as have grapes

2 We should look out for foods children crave as indicators of what they could be allergic to. ☑ ☐ ☐
Craving can give us useful indications as to what we are in fact intolerant of

	Yes	No	Maybe

3 Stress in the classroom never causes AD/HD type behaviour.

Classroom stress is a very likely contributor to AD/HD-type behaviour. Remember we can all show AD/HD-type behaviour when feeling anxious – think how anxious you feel when you are in a position when you cannot do something you have been asked to by a 'superior'

4 Attachment disorders can easily be confused with AD/HD.

This is definitely the case and, in addition, it is possible that an AD/HD child's behaviour may make it difficult for parents to parent and thus contribute to attachment disorder development

5 AD/HD is managed completely by medics and we as educationalists can have no input into its management.

AD/HD should be managed in a multimodal way. All interested parties need to work together; this means the child, parents/carers, school, siblings, grandparents, social worker, coach, health staff, which may include an occupational therapist, dietician and other types of therapist, all need to be working together with regular problem-solving review sessions where there is a focus on understanding

	Yes	No	Maybe

where the child is at the moment and moving at the right pace for the child and maximizing on the child's positive behaviours

6 AD/HD is a childhood condition that young people grow out of by the time they are 18.
AD/HD is a lifelong condition. It is a personality type. There are more and more people getting an adult diagnosis which helps them to understand their behaviour

	☐	✓	☐

7 Working with AD/HD children requires much understanding, patience and perseverance

✓	☐	☐

8 For a child to be able to learn they need their physiological, safety, love/belonging needs to be met first. *Remember Maslow's hierarchy of needs*

✓	☐	☐

9 Sometimes ADHD, AD/HD and ADD are used to mean the same thing

10 Diabetes cannot be mistaken for AD/HD.
Diabetes can easily be mistaken for AD/HD and should be screened for in the diagnostic process.

	Yes	No	Maybe

11 Good classroom practice for AD/HD children will not benefit other children in the class.
Good classroom practice for AD/HD will benefit all children

Yes ☐ No ✔ Maybe ☐

12 Some children's bodies and brains use sensations they are receiving in a way that creates disorganization and excessive motor activity.
If this is the case an occupational therapist will be able to advise

Yes ✔ No ☐ Maybe ☐

13 Cheating, lying and giving up easily on work can be seen as AD/HD-coping behaviours.
AD/HD people can engage in some very dysfunctional coping behaviours in an attempt to make things better, when in fact they often make things worse

Yes ✔ No ☐ Maybe ☐

14 When we want a child to change a behaviour we need to help them find something they can replace it with.
Always find a replacement. The human brain finds conceptualizing the negative virtually impossible

Yes ✔ No ☐ Maybe ☐

15 If we understand what sensory stimuli are needed to help a child learn we can aid their learning more effectively.
It is a good idea to watch to see how a child reacts to situations and calibrate on their behaviour so that you can help them get into the right state for learning

Yes ✔ No ☐ Maybe ☐

	Yes	No	Maybe

16 The Disability Act 2001 applies to AD/HD ✓ ☐ ☐

17 As a TA you are in a fantastic position to help young people believe in their own ability to succeed. ✓ ☐ ☐
You have a crucial role to play. You could be a one in a million

Chapter Review 3 – Quiz answers

1 AD/HD is thought to be a genetically based condition. ✓ ☐ ☐
There is growing evidence to show this is the case

2 AD/HD is more commonly diagnosed in males than females. ✓ ☐ ☐
Yes, by a ratio of about 3:1, possibly because the diagnostic criteria are biased towards boys' AD/HD behaviour rather than girls' AD/HD behaviour

3 Synaptogenesis is a process in the brain of remoulding which takes place at about 11/12 years. It is an opportunity to instil new patterns of behaviour. ✓ ☐ ☐
This is a great opportunity for development. It is also encouraging that there is a window at this age, never give up!

	Yes	No	Maybe

4 A child with working memory problems can find life easier by using a whiteboard to write lists and aid memory.
Some simple strategies can be effective

Yes ✓

5 AD/HD observed behaviour is a result of an interaction of biological and environmental influences. It is neither all learnt nor all inherited

Yes ✓

6 One gene is responsible for AD/HD.
AD/HD is caused by the effect of a number of defective genes adding up

No ✓

7 Mind maps can be a way to switch an AD/HD child onto planning topics.
Remember that the AD/HD brain quickly tires of any approach, but this one is likely to be worth a try

Yes ✓

8 AD/HD can be tested for with a simple blood test.
There is no simple test. There is some evidence that the brain of an AD/HD person shows different activity patterns to the brain of a non-AD/HD

No ✓

9 Females are better at sharing functions between the two frontal lobes of the brain

Yes ✓

10 An environment that encourages the child to remain attentive, reflect on

Yes ✓

	Yes	No	Maybe

thoughts, feelings and emotions,
exercise self-control and plan ahead
will have a positive impact on future
behaviour

11 To aid a child's concentration you need
to look for situations in which the best
concentration is gained and reproduce
these as much as possible.
*Always concentrate on the positive
aspects of a child's behaviour and
maximize on that. Pay attention to
what you want to get more of*

12 By calibrating on a child's behaviour
you can build up good rapport and
lead a child into better behaviour
patterns.
*Calibration is used extensively by
practitioners of NLP (neuro-linguistic
programming). When you calibrate on
a person's behaviour you can build
rapport quickly and enable a child to
get into a receptive state more easily*

13 Assessing when a child is in a receptive
state and choosing times to make
requests to do unpopular tasks are
helpful strategies to learn

14 Some children need time engaging in
certain sensory activities before they
are in the receptive state.
Tune into what a child was doing

before they started an activity requiring concentration and tie up performance with pre-activity. It may be that you can find a link and work out what they need to do before they start work

15 The genes responsible for AD/HD affect the way neurotransmitters dopamine and norapinephrine are taken up at the synapse between nerves.
    When a number of these genes are present their combined effect will cause AD/HD depending on the susceptibility of the individual

16 The male brain is better able to compensate for the effect of defective genes.
    The female brain is better able to compensate

17 Handwriting can only be improved by pure handwriting practice.
    Many exercises, like form drawing and brain gym, will help with handwriting

18 If a child has AD/HD they will not have oppositional defiant disorder or conduct disorder.
    AD/HD is frequently accompanied by ODD and/or CD

Chapter 4 Review – Quiz answers

	Yes	No	Maybe

1 AD/HD can appear at any age.
*Onset must be before age seven.
Sudden onset of AD/HD needs to ring
alarm bells – there may have been a
trauma/allergic reaction or some other
event which caused the AD/HD-type
behaviour*   — **No** ✓

2 AD/HD is diagnosed by a clinical
psychologist.
*AD/HD is considered to be a medical
condition and is diagnosed by a
clinician, usually a paediatrician or a
psychiatrist*   — **No** ✓

3 For a diagnosis of AD/HD the behaviour must be regularly visible in two or
more settings for at least six months.
*If the AD/HD-type behaviour is only
evident in one setting the environment
needs further assessment to ascertain
why the behaviour appears in one
setting and not another*   — **Yes** ✓

4 Stimulant medication helps the
AD/HD brain to feel 'satisfied' and
therefore calm   — **Yes** ✓

5 Common side effects to stimulant
medication include weight loss and
sleeplessness   — **Yes** ✓

6 AD/HD is not a medical condition.
*AD/HD is considered to be a medical
condition*   — **No** ✓

	Yes	No	Maybe

7 Medication can have a dramatic
positive effect
☑ ☐ ☐

8 The observations of a TA are very
important in helping the clinician make
a diagnosis.
*TAs are likely to know the child well;
your input should be considered when
a diagnosis is made*
☑ ☐ ☐

9 Each AD/HD case needs to be treated
individually.
*AD/HD children vary greatly in their
characteristics and needs*
☑ ☐ ☐

10 There is still debate over whether or
not medication is better than a com-
bination of behavioural treatment and
medication.
*But good practice would indicate that a
multimodal approach works best*
☑ ☐ ☐

11 Support for the adults around the child
is as important as support for the child
themself.
*Working with and parenting AD/HD
children is exhausting; adults need
support and understanding too*
☑ ☐ ☐

12 Being labelled AD/HD has both
advantages and disadvantages
☑ ☐ ☐

Chapter 5 Review – Quiz answers

	Yes	No	Maybe

1 Taking a step back helps to lower the emotional temperature in a potentially confrontational situation. ✔

Always try to keep your emotions detached from situations in the class-room. It is important to listen to what your emotions are telling you, because they will inform you how the child is feeling. As frequently we are made to feel how the child is feeling, however, as adults we need to be able to contain emotions and keep the situation safe

2 Consistent handling of AD/HD children is key to success. ✔

As with all children consistent handling is likely to enable much better behaviour management. Everyone feels safer when they know how others around them are going to react. Be consistent in the way you act and react

3 Behaviour programmes need to be negotiated with and individually tailored to suit the child. ✔

An individualized programme that the child feels they own will be far more successful than one imposed

4 Small, quick rewards for being on task for short periods of time will work better than long-term goals. ✔

AD/HD children will find holding long-term goals in mind difficult. This

*is a skill acquired slowly. Children
need short-term goals to help them
learn that aiming for goals is a worth-
while thing to do*

5 When giving AD/HD children
   instructions it is best to give them in
   small chunks and get the child to
   repeat them back.
   *The executive functioning in an
   AD/HD child may be impaired.
   Remembering several instructions at a
   time requires executive functioning to
   be good, therefore do not rely on this
   function, break instructions down*

   Yes ✓ No ☐ Maybe ☐

6 Building a non-judgemental relationship with an AD/HD child is essential
   to helping them understand themselves
   and improve their behaviour.
   *Working with AD/HD child requires a
   long-suffering, non-judgemental
   attitude. Coaching a child requires a
   strong trusting relationship*

   Yes ✓ No ☐ Maybe ☐

7 Always insist on direct eye contact
   when talking to a child with AD/HD.
   *Some children find this very difficult.
   Lack of eye contact does not necessarily mean lack of listening. Check by
   getting instructions repeated back if
   you are unsure. Some children find
   making direct eye contact threatening,
   some cultures do not encourage it.*

   Yes ☐ No ✓ Maybe ☐

| | Yes | No | Maybe |

Encourage it by subtle praise when it happens

8 If you act as if you are patient, in time you may become more patient.
   Acting 'as if' is a great skill to acquire. It helps you to cope with situations you find difficult by acting as if you are in the shoes of someone who can do the thing you are finding hard. Try it, you could be amazed by the results. Remember, what you project out you will get back from others

   [✓] Yes [ ] No [ ] Maybe

9 The environment an AD/HD child finds themselves in has no impact on their behaviour.
   Despite the fact that the diagnostic criteria require AD/HD-type behaviour to be evident in at least two different environments, it is clear that environment does have an impact on an AD/HD child's behaviour. Some environments will make things much worse, and some much better. Our aim should always be to provide the environment that helps the child to behave well, as during childhood behaviour patterns are laid down for the rest of life

   [ ] Yes [✓] No [ ] Maybe

10 Relaxation and yoga techniques have never been found to be of use to AD/HD children.
   Yoga and relaxation can be beneficial,

   [ ] Yes [✓] No [ ] Maybe

	Yes	No	Maybe

*but very short exercises should be used
initially while the routines are learnt*

11 Giving five times as much behaviour-
specific praise as criticism is hard but
well worth it.
*Positive behaviour management is one
of the best things anyone who works
with children can learn to do.*

12 Using very small time slots of 5, 10,
15 minutes to monitor behaviour is
unlikely to help an AD/HD child
improve their behaviour.
*Short time slots are arguably the only
way to monitor an AD/HD child's
behaviour that will be useful for them*

13 A good sense of humour that enables
you to laugh at yourself, and with
others, not at them, helps a lot in
behaviour management.
How true!!!

14 Undesirable behaviour should never
be ignored but always corrected.
*Some undesirable behaviour needs to
be ignored. Remember the behaviour
to which you give attention will be the
behaviour that is repeated, because we
all like attention. So give attention to
the behaviour to that which you want
to see more of. Unless behaviour is
unsafe it can usually be ignored*

Yes No Maybe

The Teaching Assistant's Guide to AD/HD

15 'Time out' is used to create discomfort and fear in a child.
'Time out' should be used to starve the unwanted behaviour of attention, not to make the child feel scared or uncomfortable.

☐ ☑ ☐

16 Always try to change the child's behaviour before trying to change the environment.
Changing the environment will be much easier, and that will give the child a chance to change their own behaviour

☐ ☑ ☐

17 Neuro-linguistic programming uses rapport building and sensory acuity to enable better behaviour management.
NLP is a great tool for enhancing your communication skills and enabling you to be a more active and empathetic listener

☑ ☐ ☐

18 Sensory integration is a theory of directing and controlling the input of different senses.
Many AD/HD children are thought to have sensory issues

☑ ☐ ☐

19 To help prepare a child for work find out what activities help to calm and what help to alert them to get them into a receptive learning state.
Get to know how your AD/HD child

☑ ☐ ☐

Yes   No   Maybe

*responds to different sensory stimuli
and that will help you help them know
what they need to do to prepare for
working*

20 Using the 'group mind' can help sort
    out new ways of working with young
    people with AD/HD.
    *Being able to talk through problems
    with colleagues in a facilitated meeting
    helps to find new ways of working and
    reduces negative destructive moaning*

References and useful reading

Anastopoulos, A., Barkley, R. and Shelton, T. (1998) The history and diagnosis of attention deficit/hyperactivity disorder, in P. Cooper and K. Ideus (eds), *Attention Deficit Hyperactivity Disorder.* Maidstone: The Association of Workers for Children with Emotional and Behavioural Difficulties.

APA (1968) *The Diagnostic and Statistical Manual of Mental Disorders* (DSM II). Washington DC: American Psychiatric Association.

—— (1980) *The Diagnostic and Statistical Manual of Mental Disorders* (DSM III). Washington DC: American Psychiatric Association.

—— (1987) *The Diagnostic and Statistical Manual of Mental Disorders* (DSM III R). Washington DC: American Psychiatric Association.

—— (1994) *The Diagnostic and Statistical Manual of Mental Disorders* (DSM IV). Washington DC: American Psychiatric Association.

Ayres, J. (1979) *Sensory Integration and the Child.* Los Angeles, CA: Western Psychological Services.

Baldwin, S. and Cooper, P. (2000) How should AD/HD be treated? *The Psychologist* 13 (12): 598–602.

Barkley, R. A. (1990) *Attention Deficit Hyperactivity Disorder: A Handbook for Diagnosis and Treatment.* New York: Guildford Press.

—— (1994) Impaired delayed responding, in D. K. Routh (ed.), *Disruptive behaviour disorders in childhood.* New York: Plenum Press, pp. 11–57.

Baumann, B. L., Blumenthal, J. D., Jacob, R. G., Lang, A. R. and Pelham, W. E., Jr (2004) The impact of maternal depressive symptomatology on ratings of children with AD/HD and child confederates, *Journal of Emotional and Behavioural Disorders* 12.

Best, S. (2001) The case for a nutritional/detoxification approach to AD/HD, *The Nutrition Practitioner* 3 (3): 32–7.

British Psychological Society (2000) *Attention deficit hyperactivity disorder (AD/HD). Guidelines and Principles for successful multi-agency working.* Leicester: BPS.

Buzan. T. (2003) *Mind Maps for Kids.* London: HarperCollins.

Cains, R. A. (2000) Children diagnosed AD/HD: factors to guide intervention, *Educational Psychology in Practice* 16 (2): 164–80.

Cantwell, D. P. and Baker, L. (1991) Association between attention deficit hyperactivity disorder and learning disorders, *Journal of Learning Disabilities* 24: 88–94.

Charman, T., Carroll, F. and Sturge, C. (2001) Theory of mind, executive function and social competence in boys with AD/HD, *Emotional and behavioural difficulties* 6 (1): 31–49.

Colquhoun, I. (1994) Attention deficit/hyperactive disorder – a dietary/nutritional approach, *Therapeutic Care and Education* 3 (2): 159–72.

Cooper, P. (1997) Biology, behaviour and education: AD/HD and the bio-psycho-social perspective, *Education and Child Psychology* 14 (1): 31–8.

—— (1998) Introduction: The reality and hyperreality of AD/HD: and educational and cultural analysis, in P. Cooper and K. Ideus (eds), *Attention Deficit Hyperactivity Disorder.* Maidstone: The Association of Workers for Children with Emotional and Behavioural Difficulties, pp. 6–20.

—— (2001) Medical con-trick or new paradigm for emotional and behavioural difficulties? The case of attention deficit/hyperactivity disorder (AD/HD). *Emotional and behavioural difficulties in mainstream schools,* in J. Visser, H. Daniels and T. Cole (eds). Oxford: Elsevier Science Vol. 1: 143–64.

Cooper, P. and Shea, T. (1998) Pupils' perceptions of AD/HD, *Emotional and behavioural difficulties* 3 (3): 36–47.

Dennison, P. E. and Dennison, G. E. (1994) *Brain Gym,* Teacher's Edition Revised. Ventura, CA: Edu-Kinesthetics.

DfES (2003) *Behaviour and Attendance Training Materials*: Core Day 1. London: DfES Publications (ref DfES 0392–2003 G), p. 39.

Fletcher, J. (1999) *Marching to a Different Tune – Diary about an AD/HD Boy*. London: Jessica Kingsley.

Geddes. H (2006) *Attachment in the Classroom*. London: Worth Publishing.

Gerring, J. P., Brady, K. D. and Chen, A. (1998) Premorbid prevalence of attention-deficit/hyperactivity disorder and development of secondary attention-deficit/hyperactivity disorder after closed-head injury, *Journal of the American Academy of Child and Adolescent Psychiatry* 37: 647–54.

Goldstein, S. and Goldstein, M. (1998) *Managing Attention Deficit Hyperactivity Disorder in Children*. New York: John Wiley.

Hannaford, C. (1995) *Smart Moves*. Arlington, VA: Great Ocean.

Hartmann, T. (1999) *Attention Deficit Disorder – A Different Perception*. Dublin: Newleaf.

HMSO (2001) *Special Educational Needs and Disability Act 2001*. London: HMSO.

Holowenko, H. (1999) *Attention Deficit/Hyperactivity Disorder – A Multidisiplinary Approach*. London: Jessica Kingsley.

Hyperactive Children's Support Group (2002) *Essential Fatty Acids Minerals and Vitamins and their importance in the management of AD/HD*. Chichester: HACSG.

Kewley, G. D. (1999) *Attention Deficit Hyperactivity Disorder – Recognition, Reality and Resolution*. Horsham: LAC Press.

Maines, B. and Robinson, G. (1998) *All for Alex – a Circle of Friends*. Bristol: Lucky Duck.

Maslow, A. (1954) *Motivation and personality*. New York: Harper.

Mehl-Madrona, L. (2002) *Attention-Deficit/Hyperactivity Disorder – Conventional, Innovative and Alternative Therapies for the 21st Century*, www.healing-arts.org.

Modell, J. D. *et al.* (2001) Maternal ratings of child behavior improve with treatment of maternal depression, *Family Medicine*: 691 (33: 9) 691–5.

Munden, A. and Arcelus, J. (1999) *The AD/HD Handbook*. London: Jessica Kingsley.

The MTA Cooperative Group (1999) A 14-month randomised clinical trial of treatment strategies for attention-deficit/hyperactivity disorder, *Archives of Clinical Psychiatry* 56: 1073–86.

Nadeau, K. G., Littman, E. B. and Quinn, P. O. (2005) *Understanding Girls with AD/HD*. Washington DC: Advantage Books.

National Institute for Health and Clinical Excellence (NICE) (2006) Methylphenidate, atomoxetine and dextroamphetamine for attention deficit hyperactivity disorder (AD/HD) in children and adolescents, *Review of Technology Appraisal* 13. London: NICE.

Niederhauser, H. and Frohlich, M. (1984) *Form Drawing*. Spring Valley, NY: Mercury Press.

Pentecost, D. (2000) *Parenting the ADD Child*. London: Jessica Kingsley.

Pritchard, D. (2006) Attention deficit hyperactivity disorder in children, *Clinical Evidence* 15 (June): 331–44.

Reichenberg-Ullman, J. and Ullman, R. (1996) Ritalin-free kids, *Prima Health*. Rocklin, CA.

Riccio, C. A. and Hynd, G. W. (1996) Relationship between AD/HD and Central Auditory Processing Disorder – A Review of Literature. *School Psychology International* 17: 235–52.

Richards, I. (1994) AD/HD, ADD and dyslexia, *Therapeutic Care and Education* 3 (2): 145–58.

Richardson, A. (2001) Fatty acids in dyslexia, dyspraxia, AD/HD and the autistic spectrum, *The Nutrition Practitioner* 3 (3): 18–26.

Rozman, D. (1994) *Meditating with Children*. Boulder Creek, CA: Success Booketary.

Selikowitz, M. (2004) *AD/HD: the facts*. Oxford: Oxford Medical Publications.

Spohrer, K. E. (2006) *Supporting Children with AD/HD*. London: Continuum.

Stewart, M. and Phillips, K. (1992) *Yoga for Children*. London: Vermillion.

Still, G. F. (1902) Some abnormal psychical conditions in children, *The Lancet*: 1008–12.

Tan, M. and Appleton, R. (2005) Attention deficit and hyperactivity disorder, methylphenidate, and epilepsy, *Archives of Disease in Childhood* 90: 57–9.

Useful websites

ADDISS
Registered charity providing information and resources about AD/HD for parents, sufferers, teachers and health professionals. Details of their resources,
www.addiss.co.uk

Alternative and complementary treatments for AD/HD
www.healing-arts.org/children/AD/HD/homeopathy.htm

Hyperactive Children's Support Group (HACSG)
Registered charity helping AD/HD/Hyperactive children and their families; also Britain's leading proponent of a dietary approach to the problem.
www.hacsg.org.uk

NICE
The National Institute for Clinical Excellence is developing a series of national clinical guidelines to secure consistent, high quality, evidence based
www.nice.org.uk

Neuro-Linguistic Programming and AD/HD
www.nlp4.org.uk

Therapeutic putty
Available from many websites including
www.medisave.co.uk and www.expresschemist.co.uk

Young Minds

Promotes child and adolescent mental health and related services. Includes sections to help children, parents and childcare professionals. www.youngminds.org.uk